ALVIN KARPIS
AND THE BARKER GANG
IN MINNESOTA

ALVIN KARPIS
AND THE BARKER GANG
IN MINNESOTA

DEBORAH FRETHEM
CYNTHIA SCHREINER SMITH

THE
History
PRESS

Published by The History Press
Charleston, SC
www.historypress.com

First published 2020

Manufactured in the United States

ISBN 9781467146227

Library of Congress Control Number: 2020938500

Notice: The information in this book is true and complete to the best of our knowledge. It is offered without guarantee on the part of the authors or The History Press. The authors and The History Press disclaim all liability in connection with the use of this book.

For Craig Frethem and Bick Smith for their love and support. And for Lucy Smith, Signe and Millie Frethem.

Contents

Acknowledgements   9
A Note Regarding the FBI   11

PART I. WHY MINNESOTA?
John J. O'Connor   13
The Three Rules   15
Harry "Dutch" Sawyer   19
Jack Peifer   21
Leon Gleckman   23
Tom Brown   24

PART II. THE BARKER FAMILY
Arizona "Ma" Barker   33
Herman Barker   38
Lloyd Barker   40

PART III. THE GANG
Alvin Karpis   43
Freddie Barker   90
Arthur "Doc" Barker   96
Edna Murray   103
Volney Davis   122
Other Gang Members   134

Contents

Part IV. The End of an Era
Death in Florida   139
The End of the System   146

Bibliography   153
About the Authors   157

Acknowledgements

Thank you to Craig Frethem, Bick Smith, Robert Livesey, Pam Paden Tippet, the St. Paul Police Historical Society, Fred Kaphingst, Ed Steenberg, Jeff Neuberger, Greg Brick, Charlie the Cat, Cathy Seiford, the Wabasha Street Caves, Deb Wheeler and Ted Prince. Special thanks to John Rodrigue of The History Press for having the patience to let us make this the book we knew it could be.

A Note Regarding the FBI

The organization we now know as the FBI was founded on July 26, 1908, and was then known as the Bureau of Investigation. It was not known as the Federal Bureau of Investigation until 1935. For this book, we will use the term "FBI" to refer to this organization during the era we are discussing.

PART I

WHY MINNESOTA?

JOHN J. O'CONNOR

With its reputation for "Minnesota nice," the state is not often the first one that comes to mind regarding criminal activity. But there is a good reason why many of the "motorized bandits" of the 1930s called Minnesota home. That began long before the era itself. The foundation was laid in the early twentieth century with the appointment of a new police chief, John J. O'Connor. The *Saint Paul Globe* newspaper published an article on June 3, 1900, waxing ecstatic about the new appointment: "In a few days the city will again have a police force with an experienced officer at its head."

The new chief was born in Kentucky on October 29, 1855. His parents, John and Catherine O'Connor, moved to St. Paul the following year. His two younger brothers were born in Minnesota: Richard Thomas (born on June 21, 1857), who went on to become important in city government, and Daniel (born in 1860), who served on the St. Paul police force as a detective until his death in a freak accident in 1895. When he was a young man, John J. O'Connor worked as an accountant but joined the police force as a detective when he was twenty-six years old. He soon became a well-respected and highly effective officer, solving many difficult cases and apprehending suspects for several high-profile crimes. He was known for his intelligent, logical and reasoned approach to a challenging case. He was a large man physically, standing over six feet, three inches, which earned him the nickname of "Big Fellow" or, sometimes, "Big Boy."

John J. O'Connor, chief of the St. Paul police department, circa 1912. *Courtesy of the St. Paul Police Historical Society.*

He was appointed chief of police on June 1, 1900. He worked hard to improve the department and make it more efficient. He was a popular man throughout the city because he reduced crime and made St. Paul a safer place for the citizens. There was very little money in the city budget for law enforcement, and O'Connor, who was a good cop, had to make the department run on limited resources.

Chief O'Connor had an idea to keep St. Paul safe. He called it "opposing organized crime with organized intelligence." It would come to be known as the O'Connor Layover System, even though O'Connor himself never used that phrase. He allowed criminals to stay in St. Paul if they committed no crimes within the city, and he personally made sure that they adhered to his rule. "If they behaved themselves, I let them alone," he said. But if they stepped out of line, they might find themselves locked in a room with the chief himself, from which they might emerge in far worse shape than when they entered. He and his officers were aware of every criminal who entered their city. Many criminals appreciated and enjoyed the haven of St. Paul, so they often helped with enforcement themselves. No one wanted another crook to disrupt the system.

The idea worked well throughout O'Connor's tenure, which lasted from 1900 to 1912 and again from 1914 to 1920. Violent crime was practically nonexistent. The citizens of St. Paul were happy with their police and the state of their city. Surrounding municipalities were less pleased, as some criminals used St. Paul as their home base while committing crimes in nearby towns.

Chief O'Connor retired in 1920. He died in July 1924 in Glendale, California, where he had moved for health reasons. His body was brought back to St. Paul and entombed in an elegant mausoleum at Calvary Cemetery. He had amassed an estate of more than $250,000, a huge amount of money for that time.

Good ideas can often go wrong, and the best of intentions can have unintended consequences. O'Connor's departure radically changed the situation. An article in the *New York Daily News* from April 8, 1934, noted, "Gangsters who came to St. Paul in Big John's day to behave have remained to rob, kill, and kidnap." That isn't exactly true. The gangsters who committed hideous crimes in the 1930s were an entirely new group of vicious men and women. This same article acknowledges that the system worked well under O'Connor but says that the city was now paying the price in "blood and money."

After O'Connor retired, St. Paul police chiefs changed with alarming frequency. Between 1920 and 1930, seven men served, some of them for a short time, leaving office and then returning to serve again. The last of these men was Thomas Brown, chief from 1930 through 1932. Under his leadership, the system became a full-blown partnership between the police and the criminals. Chief Brown was a true enabler of the Karpis-Barker Gang, as was made abundantly clear by subsequent events.

THE THREE RULES

Under the O'Connor Layover System, a visiting criminal had to follow three basic rules.

First, no crime was to be committed within the city limits of St. Paul. During most of the early part of the twentieth century, the rule was followed well. Robbery was almost unheard of. Violent crimes of passion, like murder and assault, were extremely rare and committed by local citizens, not by career criminals. This prohibition against crime did not apply to vice. Gambling, prostitution and illegal alcohol flourished.

Prostitution was regulated in an unorthodox manner. St. Paul officials realized that eradicating the world's oldest profession would be impossible. They decided they would control it through a system of "fines." A madam would not be arrested, but rather would appear in court monthly, where she would plead "not guilty" to "running a disorderly house." The judge would find her guilty and assess a small fine, usually twenty to twenty-five dollars. She would pay the fine and go back to work, making her appearance at the court to repeat the process the following month. In fact, in 1890, John J. O'Connor married a St. Paul madam, Anna B. Murphy.

Gambling was out in the open. Pool halls had flourished after a judge ruled in 1887 that the "risking of money" between two parties where one must win and the other lose was not gambling, but merely a "game." The Twin Cities Jockey Club, incorporated in 1887, was extremely popular. Chief O'Connor was one of the founders of the club and a frequent visitor. According to the St. Paul Police Department Historical Society, O'Connor would bet as much as $10,000 on a single horserace, at a time when his salary was $4,000 per year. His obituary stated that he was an avid fan of horse racing and that he had "won and lost" more than $1 million in the course of his lifetime.

There were classy nightclubs where organized gambling took place. The Mystic Caverns was in a cave carved out of the sandstone bluffs along the Mississippi River. One of the owners was Jack Foster, a St. Paul police officer who was the conductor of the police band. Another officer, Carl Kahlman, was a bouncer.

Prohibition, the Eighteenth Amendment to the Constitution, was the "noble experiment" that made it illegal to manufacture, transport or sell alcoholic beverages in the United States, turning ordinary citizens into lawbreakers. Alcohol was only illegal from 1920 to 1933. But during those years, St. Paul was home to several illicit bars, known as "speakeasies." There is a certain amount of irony to this, as Minnesota could, in some ways, be called the place where Prohibition began. The Volstead Act, which was the United States Congressional act that provided for the enforcement of Prohibition, was written by Andrew J. Volstead, a congressman from Granite Falls, Minnesota.

Minnesota was a paradise for illegal alcohol for several reasons. The state's northern border is shared with Canada, where liquor was still legal. That border was largely unpatrolled. One enterprising farmer in the Twin Cities, Art Peterson, started going up to Canada weekly to buy hay. Why would a Minnesota farmer need to purchase hay so far from home? Surely he could grow his own, or at least buy it from nearby farms? The truth is that he would hide bottles of fine Canadian whiskey within the hay bales. He was making more money selling booze than he was farming until one of the big-time operators got wind of his enterprise. Art's bullet-riddled body was found in a ditch midway between his home and the Canadian border in 1925. Bootlegging could be a dangerous business.

Minnesota was also home to many fine breweries. During Prohibition, these breweries were not supposed to be making real beer. Many of them went out of business, but some survived by bottling soda pop and making a non-alcoholic concoction called "near beer." But some breweries continued to make the real thing, selling it to the local speakeasies through underworld contacts.

The second rule for visiting criminals was a payment to the St. Paul Police Department. It could be called a bribe, but O'Connor didn't see it that way.

In his mind, it was just a guarantee of good behavior. The amounts were not huge and did go directly into city coffers, not into the pockets of O'Connor or subsequent police chiefs.

The third rule was that a criminal had to check-in, letting the police department know that he or she was in town and where they were staying. There were two good reasons for this rule. First, it helped the police keep track of the visiting bad guys. That way, they could make sure that the first two rules were followed. Second, it enabled the police to protect the criminals from other police departments or federal officials. During the O'Connor years, it was said that the chief kept as sharp an eye out for visiting policemen as he did for visiting criminals, and any arrest warrant from another municipality that crossed his desk was destined for the wastebasket. As far as neighboring towns and states were concerned, O'Connor didn't feel that was his problem. "Let those other towns worry. I am not police chief of the United States. I'm the chief in St. Paul. I will keep order here." However, his obituary in the *Minneapolis Star* on July 4, 1924, noted that "he always maintained that no criminal was ever allowed to stay free in St. Paul when wanted in some other city."

Of course, there were subtleties involved in the system. A lawbreaker did not simply march up the steps of the police department and announce his presence. They usually checked in with one of the local crime bosses.

In the 1920s (before the arrival of the Karpis-Barker Gang), that boss would have been "Dapper Danny Hogan." Several contemporary newspaper articles described him as the "smiling peacemaker," a man who kept criminals in line, mediated gangland disputes and served as a liaison between the underworld and the police. It was as if he took over O'Connor's role. He was considered the "Irish Godfather of St. Paul," even though he was of Italian heritage—an orphan, he had been adopted by an Irish family. He ran an establishment known as "Dapper Dan's" at 545 Wabasha Street. It would later become known as the Green Lantern.

According to Tim Mahoney in his book *Secret Partners: Big Tom Brown and the Barker Gang*, Dapper Dan's was a hot dog stand out front, but inside it was a true haven for criminals, "a place to launder money and fence jewelry."

Dapper Danny came to an untimely end, and his death is a mystery. At 11:30 a.m. on December 6, 1928, he went out to the garage of his home at 1607 West Seventh Street. He slipped into the driver's seat of his automobile, not realizing that there was a large explosive charge under the hood. When he started his car, the resulting explosion injured him severely, mangling his right hand and nearly cutting off his right leg. It did not kill him right away.

No. 545 Wabasha Street in 2019. This apartment building stands on the site of the old Green Lantern Saloon. *Photo by Craig Frethem.*

He died about nine hours later in the hospital, still claiming to have no idea who might have wanted his death. He didn't think that "he had an enemy in the world." His death was one of the first successful car bombings in the United States.

His funeral, held at St. Mary's Catholic Church in downtown St. Paul, was attended by important people from both sides of the law, overflowing the sanctuary and spilling out onto the lawn. There was more than $5,000 in floral arrangements. One attendee would later say that the priest seemed very nervous, as one side of the church was filled with police officers and the other side with well-known criminals. He may have expected gunfire to break out at any second. Hogan is buried at Calvary Cemetery under a simple headstone.

No one was arrested for the murder of Dan Hogan, and it remains officially unsolved to this day, most likely because there was only scanty evidence. Police had just a few fragments of the bomb, some of them taken from Hogan's shattered leg. According to the *Indianapolis Star* on the day following the explosion, the bomb contained nitroglycerin and was of a type manufactured in New York City. The official explanation was that it was likely done by "outsiders."

One suspect was Harry Sawyer, an associate of Dapper Dan's who took over operations at the club after Dan's death and renamed it the Green Lantern. No proof was ever found, but taking over power as St. Paul's crime boss makes for a convincing motive.

By the time the Karpis-Barker Gang arrived in the early 1930s, the O'Connor Layover System was in the hands of Police Chief Tom Brown and the three crime bosses who conspired to put him in power: Harry Sawyer, Leon Gleckman and Jack Peifer.

HARRY "DUTCH" SAWYER

Harry was born with the last name Sandlovich in 1890. Records differ as to where and exactly when he was born. Most records say his birthplace was Lithuania in March 1890. The 1910 census noted that he was born in Nebraska and was a natural-born citizen of the United States. This same document, which showed him living in Lincoln with his parents and six siblings, noted his parents did not come to the United States until 1891, which would have made it impossible for him to have been born in the United States. His World War I draft card also states that he was born in Lincoln, Nebraska, on December 15, 1890, and that he was a natural-born citizen. The 1940 federal census shows his birthplace as Russia. It seems likely that he was born somewhere in eastern Europe—boundaries between countries were often fluid in the waning days of the nineteenth century. Likely, his claim to natural-born American citizenship was just that, a claim. It was easier to get away with a deception like that before electronic records.

His draft card, completed on June 5, 1917, described Harry as being of medium height and stout build, with gray eyes and dark-brown hair. He was still living in Lincoln and unmarried. There he became involved with a group of automobile thieves. In 1915, he pleaded guilty to the use of explosives during a robbery but was given merely a three-year suspended sentence and served no prison time. During subsequent years, he lived in Omaha, where he acquired the nickname "Omaha Harry" and had several brushes with the law. He was arrested for being part of the robbery of the Benson Bank. Despite being identified as one of the robbers by two eyewitnesses, he came up with an alibi and was released. In 1921, he moved to Minnesota. There he became so involved with criminal activity that his parents disowned him; however, he maintained contact with his brothers.

Interior of the infamous Green Lantern Saloon speakeasy, photographed on May 13, 1931, as part of a murder investigation. This view is looking west toward the rear door. *Courtesy of the St. Paul Police Historical Society.*

He married Gladys Bundy, and the couple did not have any children. They lived quietly in a modest bungalow on Jefferson Avenue in St. Paul's Highland Park district. Their house still stands. The 1930 federal census shows that they owned their home, valued at $8,500. Living with them was Gladys's sister, Margaret.

He had eight known aliases. Besides "Dutch," he used various spellings of his real name, as well as "Sea Lion," Harry J. Porche, Frank James and Jew Harry.

Harry Sawyer was the ultimate "fixer" in St. Paul. His club was central to the operations of criminals who came to St. Paul. It was still the place where gangsters checked in and received all the information they needed to be safe in the Twin Cities. Harry was the liaison between the gangs and the police department, a very important and influential man.

Under Sawyer's leadership, the Green Lantern reached new levels of prosperity. Harry had worked out a deal with the Schmidt Brewery, then headed by Adolph Bremer, so that expertly brewed beer was served. Food service was added, as well as some entertainment. Of course, illegal activities continued to flourish.

Alvin Karpis loved the Green Lantern. He was quite fond of Sawyer and would later say that the two of them bonded over their Lithuanian heritage. The gang and Harry Sawyer continued to have a close relationship for the next few years.

JACK PEIFER

Peifer was born in Minnesota, which is rare among the gangsters who have been discussed. He first appeared on the 1900 federal census living with his family in Darwin, Minnesota. He was listed on the 1910 federal census living in Litchfield, Minnesota, with his parents and siblings. Although he was only seventeen at the time, he was working as a day laborer, not in school. The 1920 census showed him as a single white male, aged twenty-eight, living in a boardinghouse and working as a hotel clerk.

During the gangster era, Jack was the owner of the Hollyhocks, a fabulous speakeasy during Prohibition and a legal nightclub thereafter. It was Jack's home and business. The club, named for the hollyhocks flowers that grew around it, was in a lavish three-story mansion that still stands today, although it is now a private home. The food was served by Japanese waiters who had been trained in the fine art of food service while working on railroad dining cars. Peifer preferred Japanese workers because he believed that they could be trusted to keep their mouths shut about his less-than-savory clientele. So elegant that it had a dress code, the first floor housed the kitchen and dining rooms featuring the best porterhouse steak in town. The gambling rooms, including a roulette wheel, were on the second floor. The third floor was the private apartment for Jack and his girlfriend (later his wife), Violet. There was a large safe in Peifer's quarters where criminals could leave their ill-gotten gains. Many of the gangsters did not trust regular banks—maybe because so many of their friends were making unauthorized withdrawals. For a fee, they could leave their money in the safe, to be guarded by Peifer's doberman.

In January 1931, the Hollyhocks ran into some trouble. Leon Gleckman used his connections with the newly elected Ramsey County attorney, Michael Kincaid, to crack down on gambling at the Hollyhocks. If he wanted to stay in business, Peifer had to ally himself with Gleckman and pay him

The Hollyhocks was a favorite speakeasy of the Karpis-Barker Gang, seen here as it is today, a private residence. *From the collection of Pam Paden Tippet.*

20 percent of his profits. He continued to pay this surcharge until a grateful Gleckman eliminated the payments due to Peifer's assistance with his release from kidnappers. Perhaps Peifer was in on Gleckman's kidnapping from the very beginning and he set himself up to be the hero so that Gleckman would stop requiring the surcharge. Whether or not that was true, Peifer was keeping all his profits once again.

It was not only hoodlums who patronized the Hollyhocks. The wealthy and influential of St. Paul and Minneapolis enjoyed the hospitality and the chance to rub elbows with some of the most notorious thugs in the Midwest.

Phone conversations recorded by the Federal Bureau of Investigation (FBI) in July 1933 revealed that Peifer had his finger on the pulse of crime all over Minnesota, including the mob bosses of Minneapolis: Tommy Banks and Kid Cann Blumenfeld. He controlled the number of pickpockets in Minneapolis and was part of the operations of speakeasies all over the state. Machine Gun Kelley laundered money from the kidnapping of Oklahoma oilman Charles Urschel at the Hollyhocks. These powerful connections may have been a big reason why the Karpis-Barker Gang frequented the Hollyhocks.

LEON GLECKMAN

Leon Gleckman was born in Ukraine in either 1893 or 1894 (census records are inconsistent on the exact year). He came to St. Paul as a young boy with his parents. His World War I draft registration card described him as of medium height with a stout build, gray eyes and black hair. Contemporary photographs show a well-groomed man with a round face, a winning smile and a slightly receding hairline.

He married Rose Goldstein on February 11, 1913, and they had three daughters. The U.S. Census records for 1920, 1930 and 1940 all show the family living in St. Paul.

Leon first began his illegal operations out of the Hamm Building in downtown St. Paul under the name of the Saint Paul Recreation Company. He did offer several types of legal recreation—such a billiards, boxing and bowling—but he also could provide booze, gambling and prostitution. He was so successful in this operation that many people considered him the unofficial mayor of St. Paul. He controlled politics throughout the city and held more power than the elected mayor. He was also known as the "Bootleg King." As Al Capone was to Chicago, so Leon Gleckman was to St. Paul. In 1930, he moved his headquarters to the third floor of the St. Paul Hotel.

The St. Paul Hotel in 2019, headquarters for local crime boss Leon Gleckman during the 1930s. *Photo by Craig Frethem.*

He was kidnapped in late September 1931. Many of his associates thought it was a murder, as no ransom demand was forthcoming several days after his disappearance. Eventually, a ransom was demanded and paid. According to one newspaper account, $25,000 was raised and paid for his release, but other sources suggest that the final amount paid was as low as $5,000. Jack Peifer, one of the other important crime figures in St. Paul, negotiated and handled the payment. Perhaps Peifer had a hand in the kidnapping and engineered coming to Gleckman's rescue in order to ingratiate himself. Gleckman was released on October 2.

TOM BROWN

Chief "Big Tom" Brown loomed large over St. Paul in more ways than one. He measured six-foot-five and weighed around 260 pounds when he became the city's police chief on June 3, 1930. While he wasn't a typical 1930s gangster, Brown was every bit as criminal as Alvin Karpis and the Barker brothers. In fact, Karpis admitted that before he came to St. Paul, "my life of crime was minor league stuff." Without the protection of Chief Tom Brown, it's very probable that the Karpis-Barker Gang would not have evolved into the powerful unit that is remembered today.

Thomas Archibald Brown was born on February 7, 1889, in Nicholas County, West Virginia. Too tall to work in the local coal mines, he relocated to St. Paul in 1910 while in his early twenties. Why he chose Minnesota is unknown, but here he stayed until the day he died. He found work as a streetcar conductor until he was appointed as a patrolman in the St. Paul Police Department on August 1, 1914, at age twenty-five. Later that year, on December 26, he married Mary Welch. They went on to have five children, one of whom died as an infant.

Tom Brown was described as a straightforward family man, a devout Baptist and strict but loving father. He was seen as "all business" on the job, but "Big Tom" had big plans. He quickly rose through the ranks in the St. Paul Police Department. He was promoted to detective on April 1, 1919, and shortly thereafter joined the newly formed "Purity Squad," where his criminal instincts came in handy to encourage corruption. By 1923, it had become clear to St. Paul mayor Arthur Nelson that his Purity Squad was stunningly bad at rooting out the vice it was supposed to be fighting. Nelson hired private detectives to investigate his own investigators. A grand jury

Tom Brown, police chief accomplice of the Karpis-Barker Gang. *Courtesy of the St. Paul Police Historical Society.*

determined that corruption was rampant in the department, resulting in several cops losing their jobs, including then police chief Frank Sommer. But Brown was not one of them. He somehow managed to retain his position despite the mountain of evidence pointing his direction. His good reputation as an honest and tough police officer was restored when he shot and killed Edward Rust, a dangerous fugitive who had escaped to St. Paul. But in reality, Brown was "selective" about whom he arrested, based on how much money they could pay to keep him quiet.

In 1926, now Detective Lieutenant Tom Brown was charged in a liquor-stealing incident that also implicated his friend Leon Gleckman, the bootlegging king of St. Paul. Despite delivering less-than-believable testimony in the case, the evidence was lacking and Brown was cleared of any wrongdoing. Slippery "Big Tom" Brown got away with it again. Everyone in the police department knew better. Brown's uncanny ability to escape the consequences of his activities was a hallmark of his law enforcement career.

Brown owed much of his success to Leon Gleckman. Operating out of his offices in Suite 301–303 of the luxurious St. Paul Hotel on Rice Park, Gleckman controlled the booze in St. Paul the way Al Capone controlled it in Chicago. He was so powerful that he managed through his manipulations to get his buddy Tom Brown appointed as St. Paul's new chief of police. Soon, Brown was on his way to a private office on the third floor of the newly built Public Safety Building. Located at 101 East Tenth Street in downtown St. Paul, the new headquarters centralized all police department operations into one location instead of in several substations scattered around the city—ironically, a move that was meant to help the police fight crime more efficiently. In reality, this consolidation greatly aided Tom Brown in overseeing all aspects of the corruption within his police department.

"Big Tom" was so proud to be chief, the first one to have the honor of serving in the new building, that he brought his entire family over to see his new office. The Public Safety Building was demolished in 2010; however, the façade of the building, which contained Brown's office, was preserved and incorporated into the condominiums built in its place.

Left: Holding cells in the old St. Paul Public Safety Building, built in 1930. *Photo by Cynthia Schreiner Smith.*

Below: The Penfield Apartments in 2019. The façade of the 1930s Safety Building and Police Headquarters has been preserved. *Photo by Craig Frethem.*

Chief Tom Brown's influence on the St. Paul Police Department was felt immediately. He promoted people he liked and stuck those he disliked on the late shift. Feeling that appearances were a priority, he demanded any new officers hired be closer to his height. He dressed them in fancy, brand-new uniforms to signify his "dedication" to keeping St. Paul safe.

Under his leadership, Brown helped grow the reach of the O'Connor Layover System to new levels, with at least one-third of his police officers taking bribes. In the 1930s, crime was on the rise due to the Great Depression, and criminal activity in Minnesota skyrocketed because of gangsters flocking to the "safe city" of St. Paul. Chief Tom Brown faced a steady wave of complaints about corruption.

When the ragtag Karpis-Barker Gang first descended on Minnesota in late December 1931, Chief Tom Brown found a new and profitable partnership. Under his protection, Alvin Karpis and Fred Barker transformed their loose bunch of bootleggers and petty thieves into one of the most successful gangs of that era. The gang got protection and a safe place to plan their heists—Brown got rich through kickbacks and bribes.

A good part of why Brown was able to avoid detection for his criminal activities was that he never personally interacted with the gangsters, always going through intermediaries so as to maintain his façade as an avid crimefighter. Alvin Karpis confirmed this in his memoir: "I didn't ever deal directly with the police and politicians who made St. Paul so congenial, I didn't have to. I was friendly with the middlemen. Harry Sawyer and Jack Peifer." The exception may have been at the cabin Brown owned on Trout Lake near the town of Crane Lake on the Canadian border. St. Paul's slot machine king, Thomas Filben, had a neighboring cabin that he ran as a resort where gangsters came to relax and hide. Other cottages on nearby Sand Point Lake were used for the same purpose. Gangsters from all over, including members of the Karpis-Barker Gang, took advantage of the remote, hard-to-raid area for their vacations. Perhaps Brown made some connections there, out of sight, but that fact will never be known.

Chief Brown proved his worth to the gang on April 25, 1932, when he was instrumental in tipping off Alvin Karpis and Fred Barker just hours before a police raid on their house. Brown was awakened by a phone call in the middle of the night at his modest family home at 759 East Maryland Avenue on St. Paul's east side. It was Inspector James Crumley, reporting that a speakeasy owner had identified Karpis and Barker as living in his mother's rental home at 1031 South Robert Street in West St. Paul, just outside the St. Paul city limits. While Crumley did what he could to stall

St. Paul police officers posing in front of the new public safety building in 1930. Corrupt police chief Tom Brown's office was the top floor, far right window. *Courtesy of the St. Paul Police Historical Society.*

the police raid, Brown quickly notified fixer Harry Sawyer that cops would soon be dropping by the Karpis-Barker hideout. The warning phone call from Sawyer to the gang came in the nick of time. The police raided the house moments after Alvin Karpis, Fred Barker, Ma Barker and her beau, Art Dunlop, had escaped. Several honest politicians were suspicious that Brown was responsible for the gangsters' disappearance. Brown, of course, publicly defended his department, pointing out that the house wasn't even in his jurisdiction.

Newly elected mayor William Mahoney, having been suspicious of the chief for some time, didn't buy any of it. On June 7, 1932, Chief Tom Brown was demoted back to detective lieutenant. In his place, Mayor Mahoney elevated Thomas Dahill to be his new chief. Dahill was no threat to Brown. An FBI memo called him "honest, dumb and afraid of his own shadow." Chief Dahill wanted to fire his predecessor, but Brown had many powerful friends. Dahill was persuaded to keep Detective Lieutenant Brown, assigning him to the auto theft squad. His decision to keep Brown would turn out to be a serious mistake. Brown and his associates proved too strong for Chief Dahill's reforms to overcome. In the minds of a good portion of the police force, "Big Tom" was still the head guy, so they quietly continued to follow his directions as opposed to those of the new chief. He easily continued his rackets, garnering cash from bootleggers, gamblers and criminals like the Karpis-Barker Gang.

No LONGER IN THE chief's office, Brown rented a suite on the third floor of the luxurious St. Paul Hotel on Rice Park in downtown St. Paul. As the central police station still had plenty of honest cops on the job, his hotel office offered a nice, private place to conduct shady business away from prying eyes. Plus, it was just down the hall from the St. Paul Hotel headquarters of his good friend Leon Gleckman. Brown didn't have far to walk to collect his take of Gleckman's bootlegging operation.

The Karpis-Barker Gang kidnapping of beer baron William Hamm Jr. in June 1933 would not have been so successful without the behind-the-scenes involvement of "Big Tom" Brown, who was, conveniently by that time, head of the brand-new kidnap squad. As Hamm was held hostage outside Chicago, Brown caught wind of a police plan to hide a heavily armed officer inside the ransom delivery vehicle. That way, when the $100,000 was delivered to the kidnappers on Highway 61, the officer could ambush the criminals as they attempted to pick up the loot. Brown had the kidnappers warned of the plan, which resulted in the gang changing plans and then warning the police against pulling any "funny stuff."

Brown also led a fake raid on a home west of the Twin Cities at Lake Minnetonka, supposedly searching for Hamm's kidnappers. It was a diversion tactic to help throw the FBI off any scent of the Karpis-Barker Gang. Of course, the raid turned up nothing. Brown even argued with Chief Dahill that they should not give any information to the FBI regarding the kidnapping because the feds wouldn't give anything in return but would then claim all the glory when the case was solved. When Chief Dahill ordered Brown to pass on information to the FBI anyway, Brown simply fed them false clues to further drive the investigation in any direction but that of the Karpis-Barker Gang. When all police officers involved in investigating the kidnapping were ordered to be fingerprinted to rule them out from ransom notes and other evidence, Brown refused.

After Hamm was released, the gang gathered with the ransom money in their apartments at 204 Vernon Street in St. Paul. A suspicious neighbor, seeing all the activity, called the police. The neighbor reported seeing them carrying up a suitcase and jokingly suggested that it could be Hamm's

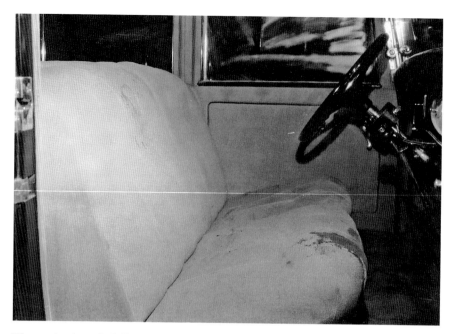

The car that brought William Hamm back to the Twin Cities after his kidnapping. *Courtesy of the St. Paul Police Historical Society.*

ransom. Chief Dahill made the big mistake of sending Detective Tom Brown to check it out. Brown came back calmly reassuring Dahill that no one at 204 Vernon had anything to do with Hamm's kidnapping. According to Karpis-Barker Gang member Byron Bolton, Brown had called fixer Jack Peifer at the Hollyhocks to inform him of the impending raid. Peifer quickly headed over to the apartment, grabbed the gang and drove them to their cottage on Bald Eagle Lake in White Bear Lake. Peifer then returned to the apartment to clear it of all evidence. Chief Dahill decided to have some police officers return to the apartment a few days later, but they found very little. They did manage to gather a few fingerprints, but Brown, as head of the kidnapping unit, made sure that it took eight months before the prints were sent on to the FBI.

He was so successful in his diversionary endeavors that on August 12, 1933, Roger "the Terrible" Touhy and three of his gang members were indicted for the kidnapping of William Hamm Jr. They were eventually acquitted of all charges in November, but by then, the trail of the real kidnappers had gone cold thanks to Tom Brown. According to Bolton, Brown received $25,000, a full quarter of the ransom loot, for his efforts.

In the following months, Detective Brown continued to help the Karpis-Barker Gang by feeding them inside information, helping them avoid arrest and warning them about several other police raids. In addition, he sent helpful tips that aided Karpis with planning their robberies, such as the August 30, 1933 Swift Payroll robbery in South St. Paul.

In January 1934, Brown announced that he was running for sheriff. The gangsters knew that having him in this position would be extremely helpful. In fact, John Dillinger's best friend and partner, Homer Van Meter, donated $1,000 to Brown's campaign fund.

With the kidnapping of Commercial State Bank president Edward Bremer in St. Paul on January 17, 1934, Brown again did double duty by portraying himself as a dedicated crime fighter while secretly partnering with the Karpis-Barker Gang. As head of the kidnap squad, Brown had files detailing the comings and goings of St. Paul's prominent (and most likely to be kidnapped) citizens, theoretically to proactively protect them from being snatched in the first place. "Big Tom" kindly supplied the Karpis-Barker Gang with all the information they needed about Bremer's daily routine. After the snatch, Brown continued to help the gang by informing them of the FBI's every move. Publicly, Brown dutifully seemed to do all the work he was paid to do by the police department, huddling with Bremer's father, Adolf Bremer, at his kidnapped son's home, discussing strategies with fellow police and FBI agents. Poor Adolf Bremer had no idea that the seemingly sympathetic head of the kidnap squad was actually in on his son's disappearance. But after about a week, suspicions about Brown perhaps hindering the investigation grew within the department. Chief Dahill had no concrete proof that Brown was helping the culprits, but Brown was removed from all the meetings regarding the kidnapping, including those at the Bremer home. This marked the end of Brown's inside help to the gang regarding the Bremer kidnapping. After three weeks, the Karpis-Barker Gang netted $200,000 in ransom money, and Bremer was released. Brown's take this time around was only $5,000 because some in the gang were perturbed that he'd not been able to feed them information once he'd been removed as head of the kidnap squad.

"Big Tom" Brown and the Karpis-Barker Gang had finally gone too far with the Bremer kidnapping. Many eyes were now turning toward the corruption in St. Paul, with Brown in the crosshairs of scrutiny. St. Paul, referred to in 1934 by the U.S. attorney general as the "Poison Spot of America," was now considered "too hot" by many big-name criminals. Most of the Karpis-Barker Gang members had fled to various cities around the country.

The corrupt Chief Thomas A. Brown led the St. Paul Police Department from 1930 to 1932. *Courtesy of the St. Paul Police Historical Society.*

After John Dillinger's death in Chicago on July 22, 1934, his partner Homer Van Meter came to St. Paul to lay claim to some Dillinger Gang money stashed in the safe at the Green Lantern with Harry Sawyer. Van Meter's value had changed hue in the eyes of Brown and Sawyer. They decided that Van Meter would be better off dead. This way, Sawyer got to keep the cash and Tom Brown could once again burnish his reputation as an honest crime fighter.

On August 23, 1934, Harry Sawyer helpfully arranged for Van Meter to be at a Ford dealership on University Avenue, not far from the state capitol, with a promise of getting his cash. But instead, the gangster was confronted by Tom Brown and three other officers armed with sawed-off shotguns and Tommy guns. Van Meter took off, firing over his shoulder. At Aurora Street, he made the mistake of turning into a dead-end alley. Brown's shotgun fired off, followed by the officer's Tommy guns. Several dozen bullets destroyed Homer Van Meter's body. But killing him did not spare Brown or the police department from scrutiny. His tenure with the St. Paul Police Department would soon be coming to an end.

THE JOB OF FIGHTING crime is often buoyed by good publicity. FBI chief J. Edgar Hoover was well known for publicizing his department's fight against criminals, often bending or ignoring the truth in order to get the political support he needed. Tom Brown operated along the same lines in St. Paul. His tenure as police chief was marked with public statements about absolutely not tolerating gangster activity in his city, while quite the opposite was true. Corruption in the St. Paul Police Department started long before he even joined the force; however, it could be argued that he was the one who brought the department to its lowest point. Under Tom Brown, corruption in St. Paul was at its peak, with the Karpis-Barker Gang one of the biggest beneficiaries of his criminal ways.

PART II

THE BARKER FAMILY

ARIZONA "MA" BARKER

Everything has a beginning. For the Karpis-Barker Gang, the beginning was a woman named Arizona Donnie Clark, born in Ash Grove, Missouri, on October 8, 1873. It was her two sons, Doc and Freddie, as well as their friend Alvin Karpis, who formed the nucleus of the gang. Who was she? What was she like? And what was her influence on later events?

Little is known for sure about her early life, although speculation and misinformation abound. There is no definitive record, but it is believed that her father, John Clark, died around 1877. Census records for 1850, 1860 and 1870 show him as a farmer in Illinois. After that, he disappears from the records. Arizona appears for the first time in the 1880 census, when her family was living in Ash Grove. The head of the household was Reuben Reynolds, who was married to Arizona's mother, Emmeline. Four Clark children appear on this census and are listed as Reuben's stepchildren.

Was part of Arizona's character and personality molded by growing up with a stepfather and a controlling mother? According to legend, Emmeline was strict and extremely religious, and this led "Arrie" to rebel against all authority.

She was a short woman, heavyset, with dark hair. Karpis described her as a "little dumpy old woman." The photographs of her that survive certainly show a woman who could not be described as attractive. She did not like the name Arizona, so she began referring to herself as Kate in later years.

In 1892, she married George Barker. Their marriage license indicates that they were married in Lawrence County, Missouri. The family appears on the 1910 census, although the name is misspelled as "Barber." All their sons lived with them in Finley, Missouri. Herman was sixteen, Lloyd was thirteen, Arthur was ten and Frederick was eight. Even though J. Edgar Hoover would later say that Mr. and Mrs. Barker were practically illiterate, the census indicates that they could both read and write. On the 1920 census, the couple was living in Lincoln, Missouri, and the sons were not listed.

Sometime before 1923, the couple moved to Tulsa. The city directories of Tulsa listed them together from 1923 to 1928. Sometime after that, they separated, and George returned to Missouri. His reasons for leaving are unknown. Some sources suggest that George was an alcoholic and Arrie simply threw him out. Others suggest that George got fed up with the ongoing and increasingly violent activities of his four sons. W.D. Smith, in his book *The Barker-Karpis Gang: An American Crime Family*, suggested that Arrie might have been going out to speakeasies and being unfaithful to George.

All four of her sons turned to crime. She may not have been a good mother, but at least she was consistent. However, only two of her sons were members of the Karpis-Barker Gang. She became infamous as "Ma" Barker, but her boys always called her "Mother," according to Pam Paden Tippet in her book, *Run, Rabbit, Run*, about her grandmother Edna Murray, an important member of the gang. Was the moniker "Ma" an example of a posthumous attempt to create a myth surrounding her character? Still, that is how she was best known and remembered.

The first recorded crime by her sons was committed by Herman in 1910. He was arrested in Webb City, Missouri, for "highway robbery." He was arrested again in Joplin, Missouri, in 1915, charged again with this crime. Arthur, who became known as Doc, was involved in automobile theft in Tulsa, Oklahoma, in 1918, but he escaped police pursuit.

Over the next several years, many arrests followed. Incarcerations for these crimes were either brief or nonexistent. But in the early 1920s, the Barker boys' crimes took a violent turn. Doc killed a night watchman in 1921. Later that same year, he was involved in an attempted burglary that resulted in the death of a police captain in Okmulgee, Oklahoma.

As the crime spree continued, one by one, Ma lost her boys. In January 1922, Lloyd was sent to Leavenworth Prison to serve a twenty-five-year sentence. Just one month later, Doc was sent to Oklahoma State Prison for the murder of the night watchman. Last to receive a sentence for long incarceration was Freddie, who was sent to Kansas State Prison in March 1927.

For Ma, the final blow came in August 1927. Herman shot Deputy Sheriff Arthur Osborn, who later died of his wounds. Herman was soon on the run. Had he been captured, he would have faced long prison time or even execution. Stopped at a roadblock on August 29, he saw the hopelessness of his situation. Most accounts of that day claim that he took his own life rather than be taken alive to face the consequences.

It was shortly after they buried Herman in Tulsa and placed an ornate gravestone over his head that George Barker left. Ma Barker was alone. That changed very shortly, as indicated by the 1930 census, in which she was listed as "Arrie Dunlop." She was still living in Tulsa, Oklahoma, but was now with a man named Art Dunlop, who was listed as the head of the household. The census indicates they were husband and wife, but they were never married, despite what they told the census taker.

Art was not much of a provider, but he kept a roof over their heads and food on the table while Ma conducted an extensive letter writing campaign to get her boys paroled. Alvin Karpis would later describe Dunlop as looking "presentable enough…a slim grey-haired guy, about a head taller than Ma." Both Alvin and Freddie quickly came to loathe Dunlop after meeting him. Freddie persisted in never using his name, simply referring to him as "the old bastard." Alvin said that he was a drunk who never showed any gratitude for all the boys did for him. As will be told later, Dunlop came to a bad end in April 1932.

Who was Ma Barker? According to FBI records, she was a criminal mastermind who turned her boys to crime, planned their illegal activities and reaped the rewards of their ill-gotten gains. Some historians still perpetuate this image of Ma and portray her as totally ruthless and domineering. Some go so far as to suggest that she ran a "school" for budding criminals in Tulsa, Oklahoma, where she trained young men on how to steal, kidnap and kill, as well as how to shoot a Thompson submachine gun.

On the other hand, Alvin Karpis said that the idea of Ma Barker as "the mastermind behind the Karpis-Barker Gang" was "the most ridiculous story in the annals of crime." He said that she was "an old-fashioned homebody from the Ozarks" and that she had neither the brains nor the inclination to be involved in crime. She was "generally law-abiding." He made it clear that she was never involved in the planning of criminal activity. Sometimes they would send her to the movies, or they would "hop in the car" to work out their ideas. It was quiet, private and away from Ma.

Harvey Bailey, another gang member, agreed. He went further and described her lack of intelligence: "The old woman couldn't plan breakfast."

And when they were working out the details of a crime, "she'd go in the other room and listen to Amos and Andy or hillbilly music on the radio."

In his book *The Barker-Karpis Gang: An American Crime Family*, W.D. Smith said that Ma "just tagged along" with the gang and "took no part in the actual crimes." However, Smith did also suggest that much of the boys' problems came from the way they were raised. He described Ma as having an overbearing personality, someone who told her children stories about the heroism of Jesse James, never disciplined them and refused to let her husband take a firmer hand. Tippet confirmed this, adding that according to Edna Murray, Ma's eyes were the most piercing she had ever seen. You did not want to cross Ma Barker. Karpis simply called her cantankerous.

Lee McGehee, former chief of police of Ocala, Florida, and Barker historian, said that she was a "fiercely loyal mother" who never believed that her boys could do anything wrong. She would defend them at all costs, believing that they had been persecuted by law enforcement. In the early years, she would accompany them to trials and hearings, protesting their innocence or at least begging for mercy. It worked too. The boys were often released into her custody. Tippet agreed. She noted that Mother Barker could never find anything wrong with her sons' actions, and she defended them no matter what.

It is interesting that all the FBI accusations against Ma Barker occurred after her death. She was never mentioned by name in any FBI records before that time. In her whole life, she was never arrested, fingerprinted or had a mug shot taken (supposed Ma Barker wanted posters that circulate around the internet are not real). She was mentioned in one verifiable wanted poster. The poster issued for the murderers of West Plains, Missouri sheriff C.R. Kelley is specifically targeted to Alvin Karpis and Fred Barker, whose mugshots do appear. But a smaller reward is being offered for "A.W. Dunlop and 'old lady Arrie Barker, mother of Fred.'"

She couldn't have been totally innocent. Karpis admitted that she at least was aware of what the gang was doing and that she enjoyed all the things that stolen money could buy. And certainly, the fact that all four of her sons were dangerous criminals tells us something about her character.

There could have been other reasons for the path her sons took, in addition to her influence. This was, after all, the Great Depression, and opportunities for young men to earn a living were few, especially for men of limited education without connections or influence. And they did fall in with a bad crowd, known as the Central Park Gang, at a very young age. Desperation and peer pressure could have had a significant impact on their future.

Gangsters were looked on as folk heroes, modern-day Robin Hood figures who stole from the rich and helped the poor. Many banks had foreclosed on farms and homes, and members of the middle class often saw the banks as the enemy and didn't really care if these institutions were robbed. This also made the outlaw lifestyle appealing to young men like the Barkers.

It was also a time when crime was attractive because it was so easy for outlaws to evade police. Two-way radios in police cars did not exist. The availability of weapons such as the Thompson submachine gun and the Browning automatic rifle often meant that the gangster was better armed than law enforcement. And fast cars (often stolen) made escape easier. Before the automobile, it was possible to track lawbreakers, who had to depend on public transportation such as trains and trolleys. The automobile gave gangsters anonymity as well as mobility.

There are literally thousands of newspaper articles written about Ma Barker's character and role in the Karpis-Barker Gang, but without exception, they were written after her death and J. Edgar Hoover's subsequent vilification of her. This may be an excellent example of how history is written by the winners. A typical article ran in the *Des Moines Register* on Sunday, May 3, 1936. It described her as a criminal mastermind who turned her boys to crime, ran a hiding place for criminals of all kinds, planned and supervised all manner of illegal activities and ordered the murder of people she didn't like. The article cited a religious upbringing: "She began with a hymn book in her hand; she died clutching a machine gun." No proof of any of these allegations is offered.

The article went on to state that there were two things Ma did not tolerate in her home: alcohol and women. The latter was confirmed by Alvin Karpis in his autobiography. He said that Ma did not like the boys to have girlfriends around, so they would often rent a separate apartment for their girlfriends to live. He also said that Ma referred to Herman's widow, Carol, as "that hussy!"—even though Carol helped Ma out from time to time and even bought her groceries.

Tippet confirmed Ma's dislike of alcohol as well. She noted that according to Edna, the gang and their girls would often get together in the evening for some drinking, dancing and conversation. But she never saw Ma take a drink.

Like a lot of people who grew up poor, Ma enjoyed the finer things in life when she could finally afford them. Although there is no evidence that she benefited directly from the gang's criminal activity, her boys took care of her and provided her with spending money, jewelry and fur coats.

She could be generous. In *John Dillinger Slept Here*, Paul Maccabee described the story of Clifford Lindholm, who was a young boy living near the Barkers in 1933 when they lived on the shores of Bald Eagle Lake in White Bear Township, Minnesota. He said that Ma asked him to mow her lawn. Even though Clifford felt that he did a "horrible job" of mowing, Ma still paid him five dollars, a huge amount of money. Ma also gave him a cream soda, which he had never tasted before. He enjoyed this treat on her back porch. On one occasion, he went over to her house with a roll of tickets for a local fundraising raffle. He thought she might buy several tickets and was surprised that she not only paid for the entire roll but also refused to accept the tickets she had bought, telling him to distribute the tickets among his friends so that they could win the prizes, as she did not need them. Karpis and her sons were always trying to get her to stop being so generous, as it called attention to the group and could create suspicion that the money was acquired by illegal means.

She was fond of animals and kept a small bulldog during her years in St. Paul; she was often seen walking him down the street.

There is no doubt that the way a child is raised is always an important factor in the direction that child will take in the future. As J. Edgar Hoover once said, "The cure for crime is not the electric chair, but the highchair." But there were other factors at work. One cannot fix all the blame on Arizona "Arrie" Barker.

In the end, she is left as an enigma. J. Edgar Hoover described Ma as "the most vicious, dangerous and resourceful criminal" of the 1930s. Melvin Purvis said that she could handle a Thompson machine gun as well as any man and was a criminal herself, not just the mother of criminals. Furthermore, he said that she reigned over the gang "like a queen." But Karpis described her as someone who was never directly involved in any of the gang's illegal activities, either planning or participating.

Most historians today lean toward the latter view. But perhaps that will never be known for certain.

HERMAN BARKER

Herman, the eldest son, was born on October 30, 1893, in Aurora, Missouri. He appeared on the 1910 federal census with George, Arrie and his three younger brothers. He was sixteen years old. Just a few years later, he was part of the Central Park Gang and then part of the Kimes-Terrill Gang, another group of toughs that took violence to a new level.

After that first arrest in 1910, he was released into the custody of his mother. The same thing happened when he was arrested in 1915.

Herman used several aliases over time, even completing his World War I draft card under the name "Bert Lavender." Released from a short prison term in Montana in 1921, he violated parole and fled to Minnesota, where he was arrested for burglary under the name "Clarence Sharp." He was an inmate at the Minnesota State Penitentiary until 1925.

He claimed to be married to Carole Antone. Census records indicate that she was a Native American woman born around 1890. She said that they were married in 1924, but since Herman was still in prison in Minnesota, that would have been impossible. No record of their marriage has been uncovered. Perhaps he was using an alias, or perhaps their relationship was never formalized at all. The couple often used the name of "J.H. and Mrs. Carol Hamilton."

Herman and his gang robbed the State Bank of Buffalo in Kansas on December 20, 1926, taking $6,000 in cash. On January 17, 1927, they robbed a bank in Joplin, Missouri, making off with a small safe. Later in January, he was captured by police while trying to rob the First National Bank of Jasper, Missouri. He received a minor gunshot wound at that time but was soon well enough to be sent to jail in Arkansas, where he waited to be tried for a bank robbery in West Fork, Arkansas.

On March 31, 1927, he escaped from jail with two other men by cutting a hole in the ceiling of their cell, climbing out onto the roof and sliding down a drainpipe.

In May, Herman and Carol took a long trip to the West Coast. Returning later in the summer, Herman tried to cash some stolen travelers' checks. A suspicious bank teller alerted authorities. Deputy Sherriff Arthur E. Osborn was ordered to track down the thieves. On August 1, based on a description of the car, he stopped the outlaw and his wife on a road in Pine Bluff, Wyoming. Herman shot and killed him on the spot.

Herman himself had not much longer to live. He died on August 29, 1927. An article in the *Joplin Globe* on August 30 described the circumstances of his death. Herman and two associates, Charles Stalcup and Elmer Inman, had robbed an ice plant in Newton, Missouri, on the evening of August 28, stealing $200. Police officers in the Wichita area were soon on the lookout. Two patrolmen, J.F. Marshall and Frank Bush, came upon the outlaws, and a gun battle followed. Inman escaped, and Stalcup surrendered to Officer

Bush. Officer Marshall was fatally shot. According to the newspaper, Herman was already mortally wounded but chose to end his own life by shooting himself in the temple.

Carol was devasted by Herman's death. She watched his burial service from a hiding place. According to the *Lincoln Star Journal*, she was arrested on September 16 when it was discovered that she had been visiting Herman's grave every night. She pleaded guilty as an accessory for the murder of Deputy Sheriff Osborne because she had been with Herman at the time of the shooting and had helped him escape. She asked the jury to give her the death penalty to pay for her husband's crime. "All I want now is for the state of Wyoming to end me," she said. Instead, she was sentenced to two years, which she served in the Colorado State Penitentiary because Wyoming had no facility for female prisoners. She died in 1962.

Lawbreakers are often thought of in terms of black and white, good and evil. And certainly, Herman Barker was a very bad man. But there must have been something in the way he treated his wife to inspire such devotion on her part.

LLOYD BARKER

Lloyd William Barker was born on March 14, 1897, and if any of the boys had a chance for a normal life, it would have been Lloyd. Certainly, he wasn't an angel, but he did not seem to be as violent as his brothers. He served in the U.S. Army during World War I and received an honorable discharge.

At five feet, seven inches, he was taller than his brothers. He described himself on his World War II draft card as weighing 150 pounds with blue eyes and blond hair, although his nickname was "Red."

He was arrested on July 4, 1921, along with an accomplice, Gregory O'Connell, in connection with a robbery of the federal mail in Baxter Springs, Kansas. He was sentenced to twenty-five years and eventually sent to Leavenworth. He was released from prison in 1938, by which time the activities of the Karpis-Barker Gang were over. Would he have joined them if he could have? That will never be known.

After his release, he tried to build an honest life. He served as a cook in the U.S. Army during World War II and was honorably discharged. He moved to Denver, Colorado, where he worked as a cook and restaurant manager.

He married Jean Wynne, a divorcée with two children, sometime before 1948, and had two children of his own with her. Daughter Eileen was born in 1947 and son Michael in 1948.

Lloyd died on March 18, 1949, in Denver, Colorado. He was shot to death by his wife, Jean. The newspapers described her as a "frail, timid woman." She pleaded not guilty by reason of insanity. She apparently suffered from paranoid delusions and had become convinced that her husband was going to murder three of the four children. She was sentenced to confinement in a mental institution and spent the rest of her life there, dying in August 1986.

Lloyd is buried at Elmwood Cemetery in Colorado. His grave marker has the following inscription: "Went straight. But too was killed by a gun. He will have judgment. He paid the price."

PART III

THE GANG

ALVIN KARPIS

Alvin Karpis looked like a typical gangster from the 1920s and 1930s. As he stood at five-foot-ten and weighed less than 130 pounds, tailors didn't have to assemble much fabric to drape him in a suit. But he had a more sinister look than most of his cohorts, including Freddie and Doc Barker. Karpis could stare right through people, perhaps one of the reasons he earned the nickname "Creepy." In later years, Karpis claimed that police gave him the moniker because his uncanny ability to evade capture during a car chase was "creepy." He preferred to be called "Ray" or "Slim." FBI director J. Edgar Hoover called him "Rat." Karpis was a smart guy by all accounts, elevating the Barkers from a loose band of bootleggers and petty thieves to a highly organized gang of professional kidnappers and bank robbers. He had a photographic memory and an ability to plan every detail of their heists with military-like precision. Karpis himself summed it up best in the opening paragraph of his 1971 autobiography, *Public Enemy Number One: The Alvin Karpis Story*: "My profession was robbing banks, knocking off payrolls, and kidnapping rich men. I was good at it. Maybe the best in North America for five years, from 1931 to 1936. My work became a profession because that's how I approached it. In another set of circumstances I might have made it to any high position that demanded brains and style and a cool, hard way of handling yourself....And I was a pro."

In its long history, the FBI has only bestowed the title of "Public Enemy Number One" on four people for being the most notorious, dangerous criminal on its Most Wanted list—every one of them 1930s gangsters. The first three—John Dillinger, Pretty Boy Floyd (Charles Arthur Floyd) and Baby Face Nelson (Lester Joseph Gillis)—were all gunned down by G-men in the latter half of 1934. The fourth and final "Public Enemy Number One" was Alvin "Creepy" Karpis, the only one to be taken alive. He was arguably the most successful. He certainly lasted the longest, avoiding capture until 1936, almost two years after the others were killed. The Barker-Karpis Gang—or Karpis-Barker Gang, as he preferred to call it—would become one of the most successful

Alvin "Creepy" Karpis in 1936. *Courtesy of the Minnesota Historical Society.*

groups of criminals in America. His choice of gang name, putting his name first, made perfect sense to Karpis—with the Barker brothers wildly wielding their machine guns, he would need to be "the brains of this outfit." Even J. Edgar Hoover, longtime director of the FBI, referred to them as the "Karpis-Barker Gang," acknowledging that Alvin was the real guiding force. When it was all over, Hoover said of the members of the gang that they were "the toughest mob we ever cracked." The gang members committed crimes all over the Midwest and the South using protection in multiple "safe towns" but most likely would not have reached their great criminal success if not for the protections and connections they enjoyed in Minnesota.

ALBIN FRANCIS KARPOWICZ WAS born on August 10, 1908, in Montreal, Canada. His parents, John and Anna, were honest, hardworking Lithuanian immigrants who had come to Canada by way of London, where their first child, Mihalin, had been born. When Albin was two years old, the family moved to Grand Rapids, Michigan, where his sister Emily was born. They soon moved to Topeka, Kansas, where his father got a job as a design painter for the Santa Fe Railroad. They later moved to a farm on the outskirts of Topeka where they welcomed baby Clara. The Karpowiczes could not foresee that their only son would soon be on the fast track to a legendary criminal career.

Two people in Topeka influenced young Albin Karpowicz's life in different ways. The first was his teacher at Banner Elementary, who, without notice, announced to young Albin that henceforth his name would be Alvin Karpis because it was easier to say and spell. The second was eighteen-year-old reform school veteran Arthur Witchey. When Witchey asked ten-year-old Alvin to help rob a grocery store, the child did not hesitate. The two broke into the store late at night, picking it over like vultures and starting young Alvin off on the career that, in his mind, he had been born to do.

Alvin then happily embarked on his own one-man crime wave, burglarizing any business that caught his fancy. In his memoirs, he recalled, "I was ten years old and already on my way to being U. S. Public Enemy Number One." Most children his age made a few pennies a day delivering papers. As a kid in Topeka, Alvin ran errands for bootleggers, gamblers and pimps, coming home with a buck and a half to two dollars every night—sometimes much more. His parents were unaware of his criminal activities. They only knew he was staying out all night, against their strict rules. His father even used a bullwhip on his son for being out late. But despite his father's punishments, he couldn't be controlled. Unknown to them, Alvin's parents were a big reason he chose to steal. He saw how they struggled as immigrant farmers. The Karpowicz family needed money, and he had found a way to provide it. But young Alvin also enjoyed the fast money and the thrill he got stealing it. He already knew at the tender age of ten that he wanted to be a criminal.

When Alvin was fifteen, the family relocated to Chicago, where he got a job as a shipping clerk, keeping his nose clean for nearly two years. When he developed some health problems, the doctor advised him to take up less strenuous work. So, he returned to Topeka to resume the criminal occupation that he felt suited him better anyway.

In 1926, at age seventeen, Karpis found himself in prison for the first time when he was sent to the Hutchinson, Kansas reformatory to serve a five- to ten-year sentence for burglary. Angry and bewildered at first about losing his freedom, he soon discovered that his time in prison would actually turn things for the better. Not because he had visions of any kind of reform. No, Karpis delighted in meeting the older inmates who schooled him on the fine art of robbery, including future Karpis-Barker Gang member Lawrence "Chopper" DeVol. The twenty-five-year-old DeVol became his mentor. For nearly three years, the two bonded through hours of conversation, with Alvin eagerly lapping up the older man's wisdom on the intricacies of burglary and safe cracking.

In the spring of 1929, Larry DeVol and Alvin Karpis escaped the filthy confines of Hutchinson by sawing through window bars with blades they'd smuggled out of the prison workshop. They immediately embarked on a crime spree through Kansas and Colorado, stealing anything they could: guns, clothing, expensive cars and more. The DeVol-Karpis partnership came to a temporary halt when DeVol was recaptured while they were visiting Alvin's family in Chicago. John Karpowicz urged his son to give up crime. Heeding his father's advice, young Alvin got a job as a baker's assistant on the north side of Chicago. But when the stock market crashed in October, he lost his job. Fine with him—he was getting bored with honest living anyway. Back to petty crime he happily went.

But Alvin Karpis was getting impatient with small, juvenile delinquent crimes. He wanted more lucrative jobs. Things did liven up a bit when his buddy Larry DeVol was paroled at the end of 1929, although Karpis began to question his association with him somewhat after DeVol recklessly shot a couple of people, including a cop. Alvin Karpis was fine with stealing, but he felt most killings were unwarranted. Not that he was totally against it. Karpis felt that he had the complete right to kill someone if they were on the other side shooting at him—even policemen, as he considered them "not so innocent." But throughout his entire criminal career, he wasn't inclined to kill unless circumstances required it to save himself.

In March 1930, Karpis and DeVol were on their way to pull a job when they were pulled over by two Kansas City motorcycle cops. When the cops discovered their trunk full of safe-cracking tools, they were hauled into the police station and vigorously "interrogated." The doctor informed Karpis that he would probably lose several teeth after the beating. He was sent to the Kansas State Penitentiary, where Alvin found another experienced robber to befriend: Freddie Barker. The two had heard of each other by reputation, admiring their respective criminal careers. Karpis took an immediate liking to the Oklahoman with sandy hair and a quick grin full of gold teeth. The two became best friends until the day Fred died. They had a lot in common but were quite different in temperament. Karpis was a strategist who liked planning jobs, figuring escape routes and running numbers. Fred Barker was smart and outgoing but had a very itchy trigger finger. In other words, they complemented each other. So, Alvin Karpis and Fred Barker agreed that they would go "into business" together after they got out of prison.

By May 1931, they were both free. Their collaboration started with petty night burglaries. Alvin Karpis knew that he'd made a good choice in Fred Barker, greatly admiring his new partner's efficiency, intelligence and ability to stay cool under fire. He was delighted when Fred suggested they up their game by partnering with Will Weaver and Jimmie Wilson to rob a small bank in Mountain View, Missouri. The first Karpis-Barker daylight robbery went off without a hitch, netting them $7,000—a small amount compared to what they would soon earn per job—but Karpis was thrilled. He vowed that there would be no more bricks thrown through jewelry store windows for a few dollars and some trinkets. Henceforth he would specialize in big robberies!

THEIR EVENTUAL TREK TO Minnesota was triggered on December 19, 1931, when the duo robbed a store in West Plains, Missouri—a job that would dog Alvin Karpis the rest of his days. When they brought his blue 1931 DeSoto to an auto shop the next day for repairs, it was recognized as having been seen near the robbery, and authorities were notified. Sheriff C. Roy Kelly was shot and killed when he came to check it out. Karpis always claimed that he was not there when the sheriff was murdered. He insisted that Fred Barker and Will Weaver were the ones involved. Following his eventual capture, authorities hounded Karpis for years, trying to get him to confess to the homicide, even after he was finally paroled decades later. He steadfastly stuck to the story that Freddie or Will was responsible. But it's important to note that he had a lifelong habit of blaming others for any deaths caused by his gang. Robert Livesey, coauthor of Karpis's second memoir, *On the Rock*, noticed during interviews with the wily old gangster that Karpis would always claim to be "conveniently absent from any events that involved deaths or murders." Livesey believes that Karpis did shoot the sheriff but had always deflected blame on Freddie Barker and Will Weaver because he had no desire to get hanged. Alvin Karpis was smart enough to know that there is no statute of limitations on murder.

In either case, as cop killers, they were too hot to stick around. Karpis, Freddie, Kate "Ma" Barker and her boyfriend, Art Dunlop, fled to Joplin, Missouri, to the home of Herb Farmer, an old Barker family friend. Farmer suggested they travel to Minnesota, where his acquaintance, St. Paul fixer Harry Sawyer, could offer them protection. Karpis liked the idea of going to St. Paul, where "the atmosphere was more relaxed and the cops would leave us alone."

Arriving in Minnesota, the gang immediately checked in with Sawyer, who went to work finding the new arrivals a place to stay. He also helped with the growth of the Karpis-Barker Gang by inviting Freddie and Alvin to

The Barker House (*on the right*) at 1031 South Robert Street in 2019. Next door is the home of their landlady, Helen Hannegraf. *Photo by Craig Frethem.*

a blow-out New Year's Eve bash at his Green Lantern speakeasy on Wabasha Street. December 31, 1931, found anyone who was anybody in the St. Paul underworld partying at the Green Lantern. Karpis would later state that he did no drinking that evening, except for coffee, so he could just sit back and watch the show. "There were escapees from every major US Penitentiary. I was dazzled." Alvin Karpis made more connections that night with high-powered fixers and experienced gangsters to collaborate with than he had since his criminal career began. For the next few years, he came to view the Green Lantern as "my personal headquarters in St. Paul."

Karpis called the action in Minnesota "brisk." While the O'Connor System did not allow crime within the city limits of St. Paul, the rest of Minnesota was fair game. Alvin Karpis and Fred Barker began lending a hand on many small jobs around the state. They broke into warehouses and stores, cracked safes, even stole cigarettes for resale on the black market. Karpis claimed that at one point, he felt like they had "cornered the cigarette market for the entire state of Minnesota."

On January 5, 1932, the Karpis-Barker Gang terrorized the town of Cambridge, located fifty-five miles north of the Twin Cities. The gang swooped into the village and kidnapped the town marshal. With the only law enforcement officer in town held hostage, they went unchallenged, looting almost every store on Main Street. Their last stop was the Gillespie Auto Company. Unable to crack its safe, the gang pistol-whipped the dealership's owner while Karpis leisurely perused the inventory. He selected a nice four-door Buick sedan to steal for the gang's getaway. They headed back to St. Paul with more than $3,000 in cash and stolen goods. Despite their success in Cambridge, other more experienced gangsters weren't yet convinced about the newly formed Karpis-Barker outfit, unsure if these hicks from the Ozarks were ready for a big job like robbing a large bank.

On February 1, 1932, Karpis, Fred Barker, Ma Barker and Art Dunlop moved into a rented house at 1031 South Robert Street in West St. Paul, a suburb just outside the St. Paul city limits. They rented under the names "Mr. and Mrs. George Anderson." Since Minnesota is full of Scandinavians, the name was pretty much the equivalent of calling yourself Smith or Jones. They told their landlady, Mrs. Helen Hannegraf, who lived next door, that they were musicians in a local orchestra. This, of course, explained the musical instrument cases full of guns they carried and why they didn't get up in the morning to go work a regular job. Helen adored her new tenants, inviting them over for cookies and coffee. She even got them to drive her granddaughter Marion back and forth to school on cold days, completely unaware that the "musician" sons of sweet "Mrs. Anderson" were dangerous gangsters.

Trouble loomed for the emerging gang in early March when two women contacted the St. Paul police to "turn tables and squeal" on the culprits responsible for the mayhem in Cambridge. Margaret "Indian Rose" Perry of Virginia, Minnesota, and Sadie Carmacher of Duluth never made it to the meeting at the police station to spill their story. Their bodies were discovered in the burned-out husk of a car near Balsam Lake, Wisconsin. The women had been shot, their faces unrecognizable from being marred with nitric acid. The next morning, while Karpis was having coffee in McCormick's Restaurant in St. Paul, he was stunned to read about the double homicide in the newspaper. He wasn't shocked by the murder; those things happen. He was surprised because he recognized the car in the photo as the Buick he had stolen from the dealership in Cambridge. Karpis claimed to have loaned the car to another gangster, Phil Courtney, and knew nothing about the murders until he saw "his" car in the paper. Worried that he might be implicated in the murders, he ran over to the Green Lantern. If ever he needed a fixer, now was the time!

Harry Sawyer was equally upset about the front-page article, but for totally different reasons. Sawyer went off about sloppiness and getting welched on. The confused Karpis eventually pieced together the story while Sawyer railed on. It seems the women had also planned to squeal on a banker who had handled some bonds for the underworld. The banker had hired someone, possibly Sawyer, to arrange for the killings but had failed to pay the $50,000 fee for the hit. Sawyer was also mad that the careless assassin had left such an identifiable car at the scene. Karpis was glad to have somewhat of an explanation and relieved that the situation would be handled by his powerful friend. Shutting up the two snitches made perfect sense to Karpis, but he was unhappy about the loss of his car—he had really loved that Buick! It says a lot about Alvin "Creepy" Karpis that he was more upset about the loss of a stolen car than about the grisly homicide of two women.

The murders remained unsolved. Also unknown is who tipped off the gangsters that the women were about to sing. It's interesting to note that corrupt St. Paul police chief Tom Brown was personally investigating the murders, even though there was no evidence they had taken place within his jurisdiction. Brown often protected gangsters, always going through intermediaries like Harry Sawyer, in order to guard his own interests.

A good opportunity for the fledgling gang to prove itself came courtesy of another important Minnesota crime boss, Jack Peifer. Peifer was also a fixer who enabled crimes and made problems go away. In fact, it was highly suspected that Peifer may have been behind the murder of the two snitches. Peifer was a close associate of Twin Cities slot machine king Thomas Filbin. Rumors were circulating that the two women were not only going to rat on the Karpis-Barker Gang and the shady banker but planned to snitch on Filbin too. Perhaps Peifer "fixed" the problem for his friend Tommy Filben by making the chatty women go away.

When the influential Jack Peifer reached out to Karpis and Freddie, they immediately agreed to a meeting at his Hollyhocks speakeasy in St. Paul on Mississippi River Boulevard. In addition to his many operations, Peifer also had a lucrative business bringing alcohol down from Canada, keeping the St. Paul speakeasies well supplied with genuine booze. Peifer explained that he'd arranged for some Canadian alcohol to be transported by train down through northern Minnesota to the Twin Cities. He'd bribed the train crew to ditch the boxcar full of booze on a side track in Minneapolis. Peifer needed a few reliable guys who could stay cool under pressure to watch out as the Canadian whiskey was transferred into trucks, just in case the police or a rival gang showed up. Karpis eagerly agreed to take on the job, excited at the opportunity to prove himself to the powerful kingpin. The job went very well. Peifer was pleased. Karpis was elated because his reputation as a trustworthy criminal was enhanced.

Freddy was inspired by the success, suggesting that they were now ready for something big. For their first major bank robbery, the Karpis-Barker Gang chose the Northwestern National Bank at 1223 North Washington in Minneapolis. (The bank building is no longer there.) Alvin and Freddie hooked up with experienced bank robbers Tommy Holden and Phil Courtney to help.

Apparently, Karpis had forgiven Courtney for the loss of his Buick. Holden and his partner Jimmy Keating had led a machine gun bullet–laden bank heist two years earlier on July 15, 1930, in Wilmar, Minnesota, a little rural town about one hundred miles west of the Twin Cities. Among the associates Holden and Keating had brought along to Wilmar had been George "Machine Gun Kelly" Barnes and future Karpis-Barker Gang members Verne Miller and Harvey Bailey.

Karpis's old buddy Larry "Chopper" DeVol rounded out the team for the Northwestern National job. To say that DeVol was enthusiastic about it would be an understatement. Declaring that the gang needed a "big car in honor of a big job," DeVol stole a luxury Lincoln so they could ride to the heist in style. March 29, 1932, was the big day. Holden stayed with the Lincoln in the bank's back alley, while the others burst in through the front. Courtney held the twenty-eight employees and customers at gunpoint while Karpis, Barker and DeVol cleaned out the teller cages and vault.

Overseeing the action in the lobby, Karpis proudly noted the efficiency and cool demeanor displayed by his buddies Fred Barker and Larry DeVol. He felt Courtney was less efficient, chatting with the bank's pretty young switchboard operator. As they were finishing up, they saw several Minneapolis police officers unloading from cars at either end of the block out front. The gang ran out the back to find Holden pressing a man up against the wall at gunpoint. It was a poor Minneapolis police detective who had been the only cop smart enough to think about checking the bank's back door but hadn't been bright enough to bring along some backup.

The gang easily escaped without firing a shot. Back at their West St. Paul house, they counted up their bounty: $75,000 in bills, $65,000 in coins and $185,000 in bonds. Karpis enthusiastically declared it was "more loot than I'd ever seen in my life!" More than ever, he knew that this work was what he had been born to do.

When Karpis proudly read about the heist in the paper, he became annoyed to learn that while one bank robber was distracted by the switchboard operator, a teller was furtively shoving $10,000 in $100 bills into his pants. Karpis was more unhappy with Courtney's sloppiness than he was about missing out on the ten grand. His need for efficiency became a hallmark of future Karpis-Barker robberies. He would plot each job methodically, planning for every contingency, spending hours obsessively mapping out getaway routes (or "gits," as he preferred to call them). He'd make the gang rehearse jobs over and over so everything would go like clockwork on the day of the actual heist.

THE EFFICIENT KARPIS-BARKER GANG began hitting banks at a furious pace all over the Midwest, including Kansas, Wisconsin and both Dakotas—using the rental house in West St. Paul as their home base. The core of the gang was Alvin Karpis, Fred Barker and Larry DeVol, with them bringing in various associates as needed.

But they soon needed to find a different base for their operations. At about 2:00 a.m. on April 25, 1932, their landlady, Helen Hannegraf, was awoken by her son, Nick, who came running in with startling news. Nick had been taking a break before closing up the family business, the Drover's Inn, a nearby speakeasy, when he decided to take a look at his favorite magazine, *True Detective*. There, on the back pages, were pictures of the boys next door, with a $100 reward offered for the capture of the murderers of Sheriff C. Roy Kelly. Most likely motivated by the reward rather than civic duty, they decided to turn in their tenants. They first contacted West St. Paul police chief Paul Braun, who suggested going directly to St. Paul police headquarters.

Nick Hannegraf hurried downtown in the family car to spill his story. Unfortunately, the first cop he approached was Inspector James Crumley, cohort and right-hand man to corrupt police chief Tom Brown. Crumley locked the confused man up in a file room and then called Chief Brown at home to inform him of the situation. Crumley quickly went to work stalling the police raid to give Brown enough time to call Harry Sawyer. Sawyer's urgent phone call to the gang's West St. Paul house came in the nick of time, with the gang escaping moments before the police arrived. They left behind a partially eaten breakfast, dirty dishes, one of Ma's fur coats, a suitcase containing shotgun shells and a closet full of brand-new clothes. But the gang was gone—along with Helen Hannegraf's fine silverware. This incident is a prime example of how the O'Connor Layover System was used to protect gangsters while insulating the police from direct involvement.

The gang was unhappy with having to leave their hideout and mistakenly thought that Ma Barker's drunken lover, Art Dunlop, had been gabbing too much at Hannegraf's speakeasy. On April 25, Art's nude body was found half-submerged in Lake Frenstad, just outside Webster, Wisconsin. He was dead of a gunshot wound to the back of the head, execution-style. There is no record of how Ma reacted to this. Perhaps Dunlop was killed by Fred or Alvin because of his loose mouth, although Karpis proposed in his book that it was Jack Peifer who disposed of Dunlop as a favor to the gang. The truth will probably never be known.

Tom Brown, their friend and protector within the St. Paul Police Department, was subsequently forced out as chief because it was suspected that he may have had something to do with the gang's easy escape. The new police chief, Thomas Dahill, was a reformer, dead set on cleaning up St. Paul. Unfortunately for Dahill, Brown had so much power in St. Paul that his demotion did little to deter his corrupt practices.

The gang fled St. Paul but continued committing robberies, most notably hitting the bank in Fort Scott, Kansas, on June 17. Ten weeks after their escape from West St. Paul, they deemed it safe enough to return to their preferred haven of Minnesota. On July 9, 1932, they arrived in the secluded vacation community of Mahtomedi, just northeast of St. Paul, renting a lovely eight-room cabin at 148 Dellwood Avenue in nearby Dellwood on the eastern shore of White Bear Lake. The gang members were determined to be model renters so as not to call any undue attention. And indeed, "Mrs. Hunter" and her two boys, "Raymond and Freddie Hunter," were quiet and well behaved, keeping to themselves. The neighbors noticed that the well-dressed "Hunter" boys would take long car rides and spend a good amount of time rowing a boat around White Bear Lake. But it wasn't for leisure. It was for privacy. Karpis had planned most of their jobs driving around in their car, the safest place to not be heard by anyone, including Ma, whom they always tried to keep in the dark.

On July 26, Fred Barker, Alvin Karpis, Larry DeVol, Jess Doyle and Earl Christman left to rob the Cloud County bank in Concordia, Kansas. They hid six gas cans along the way for the return trip back to St. Paul because cops tended to shoot holes in their gas tanks. They even brought along corks to plug them up. Thinking of how cold and hungry they would be after the heist, the gang hid sandwiches and hot coffee along with one of the cans. Karpis seemingly thought of every detail. However, the robbery went badly. After emptying the teller drawers, they demanded that the head cashier open the vault. The man refused to do so even after they roughed him up. Karpis grabbed a female hostage and threatened to "blow her in half." The teller replied, "Go ahead, she's not mine." Karpis let her go. They even threatened to burn the cashier's eyes out, but the man would not budge. By now, the back room was stuffed with customers. The gang kept shoving them in as people filtered into the bank during their forty-five minutes of desperately trying to get into the vault. Karpis decided to give up and leave with just the cash from the teller drawers. They put two women on the running boards of their getaway car to discourage anyone shooting at them as they drove out of town. After dropping off the women, they headed north. But once they were in southern Minnesota, the gang got lost, driving around in circles in the dark. They tried navigating with a compass, but it devolved into vehement arguing, as none of them could agree about how to read it. The night sky of the Minnesota farm country was ablaze with stars, so they tried to navigate like sailors by tracing their way with the North Star. That didn't go well either. Jess Doyle and Larry DeVol both claimed that they were best at reading the stars because they had been night burglars but couldn't agree on which constellation was the Big Dipper and which was the Little Dipper. The heated debate continued until they somehow blundered their way back to White Bear Lake.

Exhausted and frustrated, Karpis dumped their loot onto the bed. He was somewhat cheered to see they had netted $22,000—more than he'd anticipated from just cleaning out teller drawers. They had also grabbed $240,000 in bonds, which, disappointingly, turned out to be nonnegotiable. But thanks to their connections through the O'Connor System in St. Paul, the gang was able to negotiate a $15,000 ransom to return the bonds to the bank. Karpis was also highly amused to discover that one of the stolen papers was the deed to the Concordia Courthouse. Sadly, the cashier they beat up during the robbery suffered from nervous breakdowns as a result for the rest of his life, going in and out of institutions. In his later years, Karpis was asked during a 1976 interview for a Canadian documentary if he felt bad about what that man had gone through. Karpis called it "unfortunate," but in his opinion, the bank cashier had only himself to blame for being such a "stubborn Dutchman."

During this time, the gang started grooming more political alliances in Minnesota in an effort to cut down on local cops interfering with their work. One time, Karpis gave $4,000 to the campaign of a Minneapolis mayoral candidate, while Freddie donated $6,500. After the election, the Minneapolis mob offered them a slice of its slot machine action in return. Karpis turned the offer down, saying that slot machines were too much work—he liked stealing better. Freddie replied that all they wanted in return was to be left alone while the gang was in the Twin Cities.

After serving thirteen years for murder in Oklahoma, Arthur "Doc" Barker was released on September 10, 1932. He traveled to Minnesota to happily reunite with his brother and his Ma. Karpis confirmed in an FBI interview years later that Doc's early release had been facilitated by bribing a few prison officials. In November, Doc would, in turn, do the same favor for his childhood friend, Volney Davis, who had been convicted of the same murder.

They celebrated Doc's release by robbing the Redwood Falls, Minnesota bank on September 23, netting them $35,000. It went off without a hitch, with the gang working like a well-oiled machine. A week later, on September 30, the Citizens National Bank in Wahpeton, North Dakota, right on the Minnesota border, was robbed of $6,900 by a highly organized gang of five men. It bore all the efficient hallmarks of a typical Karpis-Barker Gang bank robbery. The crime has never officially been solved, but in the Canadian documentary, Karpis makes a quick mention of wanting to rob a bank in neighboring Breckenridge, Minnesota, the same day he robbed one in Wahpeton. He liked the idea of robbing two banks in one day but decided against it.

A newspaper account of the Redwood Falls heist marveled that the thieves had "snapped through the robbery as if it was so much routine." And in fact, routine it was. Alvin Karpis was getting bored, yearning to apply his superior skills to a bigger challenge. Karpis figured that knocking off the Third Northwestern National Bank in Minneapolis would be just the ticket to liven things up. The bank sat on a triangular-shaped block bordered by Central and Hennepin Avenues—one of Minneapolis's busiest intersections. The bank was practically all glass. Karpis reminisced in his autobiography that "it would be like working in a greenhouse, but then we sometimes did things like that deliberately, maybe to inject some extra excitement into our work."

The gang sent Ma Barker to Chicago to be away from a job that could go horribly wrong. In his autobiography, Karpis claimed that he was not at the Third Northwestern robbery because Ma started having heart palpitations. His story was that since he knew Chicago best, he was elected to see to her needs. But in the Canadian documentary, Karpis stated that he was so sure something could go wrong during the heist that he left all of his jewelry and fake IDs at home before heading off to the Third Northwestern robbery. Of the two conflicting stories, the one in the documentary is more believable. Speaking off the cuff, he may have inadvertently let the truth slip. His biographer, Robert Livesey, believes that it was Volney Davis who had been in Chicago with Ma and subsequently took her to Reno, Nevada, where the gang planned to celebrate Christmas away from the harsh Minnesota winter. As Davis had just joined the gang, Karpis probably felt he was too late to join them on a big job like the Third Northwestern. And it makes no sense that the proud Alvin Karpis would spend three months excitedly planning this complicated job, obsessing over every detail, only to sit it out. Always wanting to blame murders on others, Alvin Karpis most likely wanted to deny being present because two police officers were killed. In the documentary, when asked if had ever killed anyone, Karpis said, with a smirk and a twinkle in his eye, that he sometimes counted them up in his head. He wouldn't say how many people he had killed but bragged that law enforcement had suspected him in at least fourteen murders.

DECEMBER 16, 1932, WAS a bitterly cold day. Fred and Doc Barker, Jess Doyle, Larry DeVol, Will Weaver, Verne Miller and, most likely, Alvin Karpis headed to Minneapolis to rob the Third Northwestern National Bank. The gang stormed in simultaneously from both sides. DeVol stayed outside on the lookout with his Tommy gun. Miller ordered everyone to hit the floor, while Freddie ordered teller Paul Hasselroth to open the vault. Hasselroth tried to slow the gang down until police could arrive by pretending he couldn't open the vault. Miller didn't buy it, beating the teller with his pistol to make him cooperate. Somehow, Hasselroth still managed to hit the silent alarm as he fell to the floor. Women in the bank began to scream. A streetcar pulled up outside the window, with passengers gawking at the show inside the glass bank. The gang inside began firing, busting out all the windows and increasing the chaos. Two Minneapolis policemen, Ira Evans and Leo Gorski, heard the reports of the robbery and immediately headed over, even though it was three minutes past their quitting time, because they were the closest squad car to the scene. As the police car neared the bank, DeVol could not tell through its frosty windshield just how many officers were inside. Not wanting to take any chances, DeVol opened fire with his Thompson submachine gun. Officer Evans was killed instantly. Officer Gorski died of his gunshot wounds two days later. DeVol, thrown off balance by the recoiling gun, slipped on the icy sidewalk while continuing to fire his Thompson. In the process, he accidentally shot out the back tire of their getaway car, his beloved luxury Lincoln. The gang piled in anyway.

Behind the wheel, Verne Miller tore down Hennepin Avenue, going over sixty miles an hour on the flat tire. At the St. Paul city limits, only two and a half miles away, Hennepin Avenue becomes Larpenteur Avenue. The gang called this route "Bank Robber's Row" because it was the fastest, most convenient way in and out of Minneapolis from St. Paul at the time. The gang had hidden extra ammo and guns along the way just in case a shootout occurred. Luckily, they had also stashed an extra getaway car, a Chevy, just across the border in St. Paul. All but Miller jumped into the Chevy. They followed Miller as he careened the Lincoln a few more miles into Como Park, stopping near the zoo. By now, the tire and rim were completely gone.

As the gang was transferring the cash from the bullet-riddled Lincoln to the Chevy, the hyped-up Freddie Barker fatally shot the driver of a car that had slowed down next to them—twenty-nine-year-old Oscar Erickson, a Christmas wreath salesman. Larry DeVol, the cold-blooded murderer, was highly critical of Freddie for killing the random stranger, saying that Fred must have "been off his nut." On the other hand, DeVol had no regrets for shooting the two Minneapolis police officers. He'd already killed three cops before joining the gang. That was just part of his job. But in his mind, plugging civilians was just plain unnecessary. The rest of the gang gave Freddie grief over it too. To make matters worse, all that trouble only netted them $22,000—"a paltry sum," Karpis called it. When asked in the documentary how he had reacted to hearing that two police officers had been killed, Karpis simply replied that he "felt lucky we didn't get slaughtered." No remorse.

The gang split up, with most heading off to party in Reno. Larry DeVol, however, decided to stay in St. Paul to celebrate. He stashed his share of the loot in his apartment at the Annbee Arms at 928 Grand Avenue. A few days after the robbery, he headed out for a night of drinking. When he came back home, exceedingly drunk on gin and orange juice, a confused DeVol walked into the wrong apartment, interrupting a bridge game hosted by Haskett Burton, a telegraph operator for the Associated Press. Ironically, the group was in the middle of discussing the Third Northwestern Bank robbery. Burton had just opined that the culprits would most likely never be caught and were probably "plenty far away from here by now." And then one of the actual robbers comes barging in. Thinking that a group of strangers was in his apartment, the inebriated DeVol began shouting

ON DECEMBER 19 1933, OFFICERS HARLEY E. KAST (LEFT) AND GEORGE HAMMERGREN (RIGHT) RECEIVED A RADIO DISPATCH CALL TO 928 GRAND AVENUE ABOUT A DRUNKEN MAN WITH A GUN. TOLD THE MAN WAS IN APARTMENT 206 THEY WENT UPSTAIRS AND FOUND TWO MEN THERE. OFFICER HAMMERGREN WENT INTO THE BEDROOM WITH THE DRUNK MAN WHO SPUN AROUND PULLING A PISTOL, CALLING TO OFICER KAST TO HELP HIM, THE TWO OFFICERS WERE ABLE TO DISARM THE MAN. THE SUSPECT WOULD TURN OUT TO BE A MEMBER OF THE BARKER KARPIS GANG WHO 3 DAYS EARLIER HAD ROBBED THE THIRD NORTHWESTERN NATIONAL BANK IN MINNEAPOLIS AND KILLING TWO MINNEAPOLIS OFFICERS DURING THE ROBBERY. THE SUPECT ARRESTED BY OFFICERS KAST AND HAMMERGREN WAS RESPONSIBLE FOR THE DEATHS OF SIX POLICE OFFICERS

St. Paul police officers Harley Kast and George Hammergren, who arrested drunken gang member Larry DeVol on December 19, 1933. *Courtesy of the St. Paul Police Historical Society.*

incoherently while waving his gun. When the police arrived, they discovered that the drunken stranger had stumbled back to his own apartment. They found DeVol in his bedroom wearing nothing but socks, underwear and a fur coat. The gangster pulled a pistol from his coat pocket and aimed it at the cops. After a short, frantic tussle, they were able to disarm him and drag him out, shouting and thrashing as they tossed him into their patrol car. DeVol was like a wild animal, biting one of the cops on the wrist. The stunned police officer kicked open the squad door and yanked his attacker out with him. DeVol took off running but, as he was stumbling drunk, only made it about ten feet before the cop caught up and hit him with the butt of his gun. With the crazed DeVol finally subdued, the cops returned to the apartment. Thinking that they were just dealing with a lousy drunk, they were stunned to discover the bank loot stashed around the rooms.

Larry DeVol pleaded guilty to the murders of the two Minneapolis police officers, receiving a sentence of life in prison, thus ending his long association with Alvin Karpis. The warden at the Stillwater prison was disturbed by the behavior of his new, cold-blooded prisoner. DeVol's wanted poster had been correct when it described him as "paranoid and delusional" and willing to kill anyone without provocation. DeVol was eventually declared insane after he accused guards of injecting poisonous gas into his cell. He was transferred to a hospital for the criminally insane in St. Peter, Minnesota.

KARPIS FIGURED THAT HIS next job would be in Fairbury, Nebraska. He did his research well, always robbing rural banks during the times when they would be loaded with more cash for the farmers: spring planting, wheat harvest and so on. Around the end of February, the gang moved back to the safer, more pleasant confines of St. Paul to finish planning the heist, checking into the Grand Avenue Apartments at 1290 Grand Avenue. Unfortunately, in March, they again had to scram when tipped off by Harry Sawyer about an upcoming police raid.

The gang robbed the Fairbury, Nebraska bank on April 4, 1933. The eight guys on the job were Karpis, both Barker brothers, Jess Doyle, Earl Christman, Frank Nash, Eddie Green and Volney Davis. It was a rough one—eight innocent bystanders were wounded during the gun battle. Earl Christman took a bullet through the collar bone. Karpis considered it a success despite all the shooting, as the gang netted $37,000 cash and $39,000 in bonds—plus nobody died. But he spoke too soon. Christman was taken to Verne Miller's place in Kansas City, where friendly doctors willing to keep mum were harder to find than in St. Paul. Karpis and Green did some home doctoring, mostly consisting of morphine shots. When a doctor finally did show up, Christman stood up to prove how well he was recovering but, in doing so, reopened his wound and bled to death. Christman was quickly buried in an unmarked grave somewhere near Kansas City. Karpis and the gang had no time to be sentimental about funerals or notifying next of kin. That kind of stuff got you caught.

Upon return to St. Paul, they were quickly summoned to the Hollyhocks by Jack Peifer. Fred and Alvin sat in Peifer's office while he laid out a request for a new venture: a kidnapping.

Karpis was reluctant at first. Kidnapping was not something he'd considered. He'd put a lot of thought into his criminal choices. He liked being a thief. He didn't want to do murder for hire—too messy. And the rackets, well, that got you involved with the mob. Not that he minded the mob, it's just that it wouldn't allow him to continue stealing while in its employ. But the kidnapping became more attractive when Peifer starting talking money. The gang would net $90,000 after paying Peifer his cut. Now Karpis was all in. He was so excited that he forgot to ask who the intended victim was until halfway out the door. Karpis approved of the choice when informed that he was to snatch William Hamm Jr., president of Hamm's Brewery in St. Paul. While Prohibition had been repealed, it wasn't completely gone— that wouldn't happen until December 5, 1933. Restrictions on alcohol were being lifted one step at a time. Since 3.2 beer was again legal, Karpis knew that Hamm's Brewery would be flush with cash from supplying the suds to a thirsty population denied real beer for more than thirteen years. In retrospect, thinking about just how much money the brewery was raking in, Karpis began to wonder why the ransom wasn't bigger. He suspected that maybe it really had to do with more than money—maybe there was something political about it. His hunch may have been correct. There is some speculation that the kidnapping was a message for the new law-and-order police chief Thomas Dahill, who had been arresting gangsters in St. Paul despite the O'Connor Layover agreement. Perhaps a high-profile crime within his city limits might make the chief honor those unwritten rules.

Peifer rented the gang a cottage called Idlewild on Bald Eagle Lake in White Bear Lake just north of St. Paul. It was a lovely, secluded place for Alvin Karpis to start planning the biggest job of his career. He made almost daily trips to St. Paul to study Hamm's habits, to figure out the best time and place for the kidnapping. He mostly cased the Hamm's Mansion at 671 Cable Avenue (now Greenbrier Street) and the brewery down the hill at Minnehaha and Payne Avenues. Karpis wrote later that after doing so much research on Hamm, he "was sick of him long before the kidnapping." They finally settled on grabbing Hamm as he walked home from the brewery to have lunch, which the brewer did every day at the same time.

But there were many details yet to be planned before the kidnapping could take place. It was a massive operation. Karpis knew that while he was a master at engineering bank heists, this was something else. He needed some more brainpower and muscle. Peifer sent word to Chicago asking to borrow a few guys for the job. Sent along to Minnesota to help were Capone syndicate gang members "Shotgun" George Ziegler and Byron Bolton, both veterans of the infamous 1929 St. Valentine's Day Massacre. Ziegler took credit for engineering many details of the massacre, such as arriving in a vehicle dressed up to look like a patrol car.

Ziegler rented a house from the postmaster in the Chicago suburb of Bensenville to use as the place to hide Hamm. Karpis liked the idea, reasoning that no one would think to look for a kidnap victim in the home of the postmaster. On their way back to St. Paul, they hid three gas cans along the way in various Wisconsin cornfields. Unlike during a bank robbery, these cans were not in case cops shot holes in their gas tank. If all went according to plan, they would get clean away before anyone could chase after them. However, since there was no such thing as self-service gas back then, the gang really couldn't stop at the service station to fill up with their victim tied up in the back seat. They couldn't take any chances with some nosy Nellie gas station attendant getting curious.

June 15, 1933, was the big day. As William Hamm walked home for lunch at 12:45 p.m., a big limousine pulled up next to him. Charlie Fitzgerald got out and approached Hamm. Karpis chose Fitzgerald to be the "greeter" because at fifty-seven years old, with gray hair and a distinguished mustache, Charlie looked like just another businessman wishing to have a conversation. Hamm would have no reason to suspect Fitzgerald posed any danger, as gangsters were mostly younger guys under age thirty-five. Karpis was driving the car wearing a chauffeur's cap to further lend credence to the façade. Looking back, Karpis proudly called the execution of his plan "a masterpiece!" Fitzgerald walked up to Hamm with his hand extended, saying, "Mr. Hamm, I wonder if I might speak to you on a rather important business matter." Completely unsuspecting, Hamm shook his hand. Instead of letting go, Fitzgerald gently guided Hamm to the car and slipped him into the back seat. Karpis was amazed that Hamm did not seem to comprehend that he was being kidnapped when Bolton and Doc slid into the car too, causing the brewer to be sandwiched in between Bolton and Fitzgerald. When Charlie Fitzgerald politely asked Hamm to crouch down on the floorboards, he quietly did so without questioning why. Karpis, who had an obsessive need for every step of his plans to be followed to the letter, was concerned. Fitzgerald had skipped a step by not waiting as instructed for Hamm to respond before snatching him. As they drove away, Karpis wondered aloud if they'd gotten the right man as the victim had not confirmed his identity first. Hearing the discussion, Hamm helpfully spoke up from the floor boards, assuring them that he was indeed William Hamm Jr. It seems strange that Karpis would doubt that fact since he had just spent many weeks watching Hamm and should have easily recognized his victim.

Twenty minutes later, they arrived at their getaway car, stashed just outside St. Paul. The transfer went smoothly. Hamm signed the prepared ransom notes without objection. With Hamm blindfolded, they headed for Bensenville. Karpis stayed with Hamm the entire time, calling him a "model prisoner" and "an okay guy." Karpis liked him so much that he did whatever he could to make his "guest" comfortable: setting up fans to cool off the hot room and bringing him books and the *Saturday Evening Post* to read. "Creepy" Karpis even kindly reassured the brewery president that he would be released soon when Hamm fussed about being away from his business during a busy time. The room was so stifling warm that Karpis even offered Hamm a refreshing beer. Unfortunately, there was no Hamm's beer in the house, so he had to serve his new friend a different brand, a situation that caused Karpis to fret. It's a look into the strange mind of Alvin Karpis that he thought it fine to terrorize the man by kidnapping him, extorting him for ransom and possibly harming or even killing him if necessary—but serving him a competitor's beer was a terrible faux pas. Karpis was so worried about offending Hamm that he took the time to scrape the labels off the bottle, even asking Hamm if he could tell what kind of beer he was drinking. The genial victim replied, "I always say Hamm's is the best, but to tell you the truth, I don't know what the hell brand this is." Of course, it's also possible that Karpis removed the labels from the locally brewed beer because he did not want Hamm to know he was being held near Chicago.

The day after the kidnapping, George Ziegler left the ransom note in a booth at the Rosedale Pharmacy at 1941 Grand Avenue in St. Paul. After a few bumps, the $100,000 ransom was paid. Sitting in Bensenville, the gang was delirious with joy at having pulled it off. According to Karpis, "We whooped and hollered as we opened up the briefcase and spread out the money." Ziegler crowed, "You better round up some Hamm's beer, I got a feeling that it'll be my favorite brand for a long time to come!"

It was during this time that Karpis learned his friend Frank Nash had been killed in a failed attempt led by Verne Miller to spring him from federal custody in Kansas City. Karpis had contributed money to help fund the operation. While he thought Nash's death a shame, Karpis was quite upset to hear that a federal agent and two cops were killed. Not that he felt bad for the dead officers—as usual, he was more worried about how things affected him. Annoyingly, this meant there would be even more FBI agents in the Midwest, combing for the perpetrators of what became known as the Kansas City Massacre. Because of this, Karpis decided to not drop Hamm off in St. Paul, as originally planned, instead opting for a remote cornfield more than thirty miles north in Wyoming, Minnesota. While Hamm bathed for the trip home, Karpis slipped a few twenties from the ransom money into Hamm's wallet. Not because Alvin was a thoughtful guy, but because he was smart enough to think of every detail that might possibly get them caught.

St. Paul police investigating in front of the Hamm's Mansion shortly after the kidnapping.
Courtesy of the St. Paul Police Historical Society.

He wanted Hamm to spend the bills before they did. Karpis reasoned that if the newspapers reported that some of the ransom money had been spent in St. Paul, this would tell him the money was marked. Hamm was released on the morning of June 19, after three and a half days of captivity. Feeling a bit bad about dumping Hamm in the middle of nowhere, Karpis even handed him a ham sandwich to eat while passing the time. He requested that Hamm please sit and wait an hour or so before making any phone calls. Hamm politely agreed, reassuring the nice fellow that he didn't think he could identify any of them anyway.

Karpis headed back to Chicago to drop off Byron Bolton, while Fred and a few others stayed in St. Paul, taking the ransom money to their apartments at 204 Vernon Street. When an alert citizen called the police to report suspicious activity around the building, Detective Tom Brown warned the gang, helping them once again to evade capture. Brown had been very helpful during Hamm's kidnapping, diverting suspicion from the Karpis-Barker Gang by feeding false clues to the FBI to the point that Roger "the Terrible" Touhy and his gang were charged with the crime—a fact that tickled Karpis to no end. He had no beef with the Touhy Gang but didn't care one bit that they were sitting in jail for a crime he had committed. At the time, the FBI was still unaware that the Karpis-Barker Gang even existed—and Karpis liked it that way. The Touhy Gang even went to trial for the kidnapping that November. But without solid evidence, they were acquitted. The search for the real kidnappers resumed, but by then, the trail was cold, with Detective Brown happily doing what he could to gum up the investigations. After his capture, Byron Bolton supplied the FBI with a breakdown of how the ransom money had been distributed. The list alleges that Detective Tom Brown received $25,000, one quarter of the ransom. The large amount may not have been completely due to the Karpis-Barker

November 13, 1933. The Touhy Gang poses in the Ramsey County jail while awaiting trial for the kidnapping of William Hamm Jr. *From left to right*: unknown deputy sheriff, Eddie "Chicken Micky" McFadden, Roger "the Terrible" Touhy, Gustave "Gloomy Gus" Schaefer and Willie Sharkey. *Courtesy of the St. Paul Police Historical Society.*

Gang's deep gratitude for the policeman's help. Brown may have required this lion's share of the loot in order to pay off a lot of other crooked people to look the other way after the gang committed the kidnapping within the St. Paul city limits, going against the O'Connor System. This resulted in the Karpis-Barker Gang netting less from the ransom than the $90,000 promised by Jack Peifer.

THE GANG REUNITED BACK in Minnesota to pull off a payroll robbery on August 30, 1933, in South St. Paul, a suburb just outside the St. Paul city limits. This robbery once again exhibited the gang's prowess for efficiency and speed. Karpis had planned out every step of the operation, as usual, having the gang rehearse it all ahead of time. Karpis brought Charlie Fitzgerald, Byron Bolton and George Ziegler back from Chicago since they'd all worked so well together on the Hamm kidnapping. He chose the thirtieth because it would net a greater amount of cash than the mid-month payroll. And indeed, it was actual money, not checks. In 1933, there was not yet any such thing as Social Security tax or Minnesota state income tax, so most people were still paid in good old untraceable cash. The Swift Packing Company sent its payroll down by rail from the Federal Reserve Bank in Minneapolis to the South St. Paul Post Office. From there, it would be taken down the block to the Livestock Exchange Building, closely guarded all the way.

Alvin Karpis sat behind the wheel of their heavily armored getaway car, Doc Barker next to him with a sawed-off shotgun hidden up the sleeve of his coat. Taking a page from Ziegler's Valentine's Day Massacre, the getaway car was altered to look like a police car. Adding to the ruse, Karpis's chauffeur cap could easily be mistaken for a policeman's cap. Freddie Barker stood across the street with his Tommy gun wrapped in a newspaper, ironically containing stories about the Hamm kidnapping. Two more gang members hung out in a nearby café. South St. Paul police officer John Yeaman sat behind the wheel of his patrol car positioned in the alley between the post office and the cafe. The cash came out the front door, guarded by Yeaman's partner, Officer Leo Pavlak, along with two Swift payroll employees. Karpis rolled up the fake patrol car, which was purposely belching smoke to add to the confusion. Doc jumped out to confront Pavlak, forcing the officer to drop his gun and raise his hands. The two Swift guards immediately dropped the cash bags and rolled under their truck. Officer Yeaman, sensing the commotion, started to slowly pull his patrol car forward to peek around to the front of the post office. Seeing the real police

Livestock Exchange Building in 2019. The Swift Packing Company payroll was supposed to be delivered here but was stolen by the Karpis-Barker Gang in 1933. *Photo by Craig Frethem.*

car, Doc screamed at Officer Pavlak, "You dirty rat, son of bitch!" and fired his shotgun at the policeman's head. Officer Leo Pavlak, a thirty-eight-year-old father of two who had only been a policeman for four months, died instantly. Meanwhile, Freddie opened fire with his Tommy gun on the patrol car, spraying Officer Yeaman repeatedly through the windshield. Fred then reached in and dragged the officer out of the way so he could help himself to the policeman's Tommy gun resting on the passenger seat. Despite having twenty-five bullet fragments in his head and neck and being tossed down the alley like a sack of potatoes, Yeaman survived—although he was blinded in one eye. When he died in 1971, he still had many pieces of lead from Fred Barker's Tommy gun in his head and neck.

By now, bullets were flying everywhere. Fred stood in the middle of the street swinging his Thompson in a circle while firing to keep the crowd back. Guards busted out the windows on the top floor of the post office, shooting at the street. Bullets were found in houses blocks away. Charlie Fitzgerald, shot through the hip, had to be dragged into the getaway car. The gang quickly sped up Concord Boulevard toward the safety and protection of the St. Paul city limits while tossing out roofing tacks and other sharp objects through a special hole in the floorboards to give anyone

The South St. Paul Post Office in 2019. *Photo by Craig Frethem.*

who chased them a flat tire. It was over in less than two minutes due to Karpis's efficient planning. Their haul was $33,000. The robbery was so violent that even other gangsters condemned it. In his book, Alvin Karpis expressed no regrets. The only sympathy he conjured up was for "poor Chuck," fretting about how long it took Fitzgerald to heal because of his age. Karpis summed up the crime in which one policeman was executed and the other disabled for life as "a good day's work."

ALVIN KARPIS WENT TO Chicago to wait for Minnesota to cool down. He loved Minnesota—he hated Chicago. It gave "Creepy" the creeps. Too many buildings, not enough prairie. He liked making his escapes down vast country roads surrounded by cornfields. Perhaps it was because of his restlessness that he allowed George Ziegler to talk him into robbing the Chicago Federal Reserve. Karpis did his usual diligence, planning every meticulous detail. The robbery went off without a hitch on September 22, 1933—until the gang crashed the car during the getaway. Nearby cops came running. Doc Barker and Byron Bolton, ever the hotheads who shot first and thought later, immediately started firing blindly from inside their car. Bolton accidentally shot Doc in the hand but kept spraying his machine gun anyway. They stole another car and made it back to their Elmhurst hideout. Karpis was furious. The gang had sunk a lot of money into armoring that Hudson, only to leave it behind along with a lot of ammo and, most likely, several fingerprints. Doc was hopping mad about his hand getting shot, not because of his grazing wound but because Bolton had managed to shoot the huge diamond out of his favorite ring. Things got even worse when they tore open the canvas bags. Every single one of them was stuffed with useless canceled checks. All of that expense and labor had been for absolutely nothing. Karpis's mood got even worse the next day when he read that Bolton's reckless shooting had killed Chicago policeman Miles Cunningham. Of course, Karpis was not upset about the death of a cop, just annoyed with all the careless mistakes and extra scrutiny brought on by killing a policeman. In his book, Karpis predictably claimed that he wasn't along on that job, electing to sit out because it was determined that only five guys were needed to pull it off. It's an unlikely story. In his later years, Alvin Karpis had a way of bending stories to blame any deaths on other gang members who couldn't defend themselves, as they were conveniently dead.

Between their expenses and netting nothing on the caper, the gang was having a cash flow problem. Karpis headed to St. Paul to borrow some money from Harry Sawyer and Jack Peifer. Ever full of pride, Karpis was extremely glad that he was not the type to boast about his jobs like the clumsy Machine Gun Kelly or that weird couple Bonnie and Clyde. He was happy that Sawyer, and especially Peifer, whom he didn't completely trust, wouldn't know that his gang was the one involved in the violent and fruitless Chicago Federal Reserve job. But the wily Peifer somehow knew anyway. Sitting in his lavish office at the Hollyhocks, Peifer took great delight in rubbing the failure in Alvin Karpis's proud face. Karpis tried to play dumb but soon realized it was no good. Peifer laughingly told him that if he'd just asked around, he would have discovered that another gang had tried the exact same thing two years earlier with equal results. Karpis's connections in Chicago had proven less informative than what he enjoyed in St. Paul.

Angry and frustrated, Karpis headed back to Chicago, where Freddie was still plenty mad at Ziegler for suggesting the whole fiasco. Karpis only expressed regret that he would now have to wait before implementing his next big move: immigrating to Australia. It took Fred a few minutes to figure out that his friend was not joking. Karpis explained: "This country is going to get real hot for me." When Fred finally realized that his best friend was serious, Karpis predicted, "Freddie, we just don't have that much time left."

CHICAGO NEWSPAPERS WERE SCREAMING headlines that ten thousand police were searching for the cop killers from the Federal Reserve job. The gang decided to return to Minnesota, where things were friendlier. Whether it was because of his need for cash or his love of pulling off a big caper, Alvin Karpis agreed to another kidnapping, against his better judgment. At first, the gang had planned to rob the Commercial State Bank, but Harry Sawyer argued that they should kidnap the bank's president, Edward Bremer, instead. Karpis couldn't figure out why Sawyer was so adamant about it. Perhaps it was another message to Chief Dahill. Or maybe it was because Ed Bremer's father was Adolph Bremer, president of the Schmidt Brewery, which had continued to brew beer illegally during Prohibition, selling it to customers like the Green Lantern—for the right price. Maybe Sawyer was getting even for some price gouging by the brewery now that Prohibition had come to an end. In fact, Sawyer's wife, Gladys, later told the FBI that her husband and the Bremers had once had "some differences" over alcohol.

Karpis was initially reluctant for many reasons. First, the FBI would get involved now that the Lindbergh law had made kidnapping a federal crime. (The law was prompted by the 1932 kidnapping of Charles Lindbergh Jr., the twenty-month-old son of the famous Minnesota aviator; the baby had been found dead.) Secondly, the Bremer family was good friends and supporters of President Franklin Roosevelt, a fact that would surely prompt the feds to get involved even more. Freddie had no such misgivings, instantly liking the whole idea. Ziegler didn't care for it at all either, but like Karpis, he was persuaded by the proposed $200,000 ransom. Ziegler had blown his share of the Hamm ransom playing the commodities market. He told Sawyer, "Yeah I'll go on the damn thing." Along with Ziegler, Freddie and Karpis, the team was rounded out with Doc Barker, Will Weaver, Volney Davis and Harry Campbell.

The gang set about planning the job, splitting time between two St. Paul apartments: Freddie's on the corner of Dale and Grand and Will Weaver and Myrtle Eaton's place at the Kennington Apartments at 565 Portland Avenue. The planning process was a lot easier than with William Hamm, as Detective Tom Brown, still head of the kidnap squad, was able to provide Karpis with detailed information on Bremer's daily routines. The squad had been ordered to collect information on prominent citizens to protect them from just the kind of thing that Brown was helping the Karpis-Barker Gang to do.

But despite the relative ease of planning, Karpis couldn't shake the feeling that the job was a mistake. In fact, Edna Murray, Volney Davis's girlfriend, later reported that the whole gang was on edge. Those nerves led to a serious incident on January 13, 1934. At about 1:00 a.m., during one of their meetings at the Kennington, they noticed a guy peeking into the windows of the Holly Falls Apartments across the alley. Worried that they had somehow been discovered, Fred and Alvin tore out the building to investigate. As they drove their Chevy around the surrounding streets, a Ford coupe slowed down to look at them. Inside, they saw two men in blue uniforms with gold buttons and peaked hats—cops! Karpis jumped out, firing his Tommy gun into the Ford, hitting the driver. He unloaded almost fifty bullets, making sure that those cops wouldn't be following them anymore. Reading the newspaper the next morning, Karpis discovered that he had made a serious error. The man he shot was Roy McCord, a radio operator for Northwest Airways. McCord's wife had been expressing concern about a peeping Tom in the neighborhood. Seeing the gang's unfamiliar car the day before, McCord had followed them as they approached the Kennington in an effort to catch the peeper. That night, McCord had enlisted a co-worker to come home with him, neither of them bothering to change out of their airline uniforms. McCord was seriously wounded but did survive.

Karpis was anxious. The whole Bremer job felt like "one giant-sized jinx." He opted to delay the kidnapping a few days until the frenzy over the McCord fiasco died down. The gang had planned to snatch Bremer in downtown St. Paul as he walked through Rice Park to his office in the Commercial State Bank, right next door to the St. Paul Hotel. But then Karpis got word from his police informants that Bremer had inexplicably fired the bodyguard who usually escorted him through the park. This should have made things easier, but Karpis was jittery about it. The unexpected made him nervous. He changed his plans. Every morning, Ed Bremer left his beautiful St. Paul mansion at 92 North Mississippi River Boulevard to drive his eight-year-old daughter, Betty, off to the Summit School for girls at 1150 Goodrich Avenue (today known as St. Paul Academy and Summit School, having merged with the all-boy school in 1969). After his young daughter safely entered the school, Bremer drove his Lincoln one block east on Goodrich to the stop sign at Lexington Avenue.

Karpis eased his car behind Bremer's sedan while Fred Barker and Harry Campbell, driving south on Lexington, slammed their car to a stop in front. Bremer was boxed in, unable to move his vehicle. Doc Barker and Volney Davis flew out of Karpis's car, wrenched open Bremer's doors and shoved a gun in the surprised banker's face. Right from the start, it was obvious that Bremer would not be the docile, compliant fellow William

Summit School, currently the St. Paul Academy and Summit School. Edward Bremer dropped off his eight-year-old daughter, Betty, here just before he was kidnapped by the Karpis-Barker Gang. *Photo by Craig Frethem.*

Hamm had been. Bremer struggled to escape. Doc pushed him back into the car, whacking at the banker's head with the butt of his gun. Davis jumped into the driver's seat. Bremer's legs were hanging out the door, and he refused to bring them into the car. The kidnappers had no time for that—they slammed the door anyway, causing serious injury to his knee. Curled up on the floorboards, Bremer feared for his life as Doc, never one to keep his anger in check, continued to beat him on the head. Davis eventually got Bremer's Lincoln started, and the caravan of three vehicles sped south on Lexington. They dumped Bremer's car two miles away near the Highland Park Golf Course, continuing on to the getaway car stashed just outside the city limits. As with Hamm, their hostage was immediately given ransom notes to sign. Bremer had trouble doing so because of all the blood gushing from the head wounds inflicted on him by the butt of hot-tempered Doc Barker's gun.

With Bremer subdued and blindfolded in the back seat, Alvin Karpis, Volney Davis and Doc Barker hit the open road for Bensenville, Illinois—apparently George Ziegler's favorite place to stash a kidnap victim. The gang had once again hidden gas cans along the way to avoid curious filling

Exterior of Edward Bremer's car. *Courtesy of the St. Paul Police Historical Society.*

station attendants. Freddie and Ziegler stayed in St. Paul to deliver the ransom notes. With Bremer safely delivered to a farmhouse in Illinois, Davis headed back to St. Paul to get his girlfriend, Edna Murray.

Edward Bremer was not the model prisoner that William Hamm had been. Alvin Karpis, once again in charge of guarding their captive, called him "just naturally a slightly miserable bastard." Bremer complained nonstop the entire time: about the food, the heat, the wound on his head and so forth. Bremer fussed about them stealing his watch or his wallet, expressing disbelief that his family would cough up the $200,000 ransom. Bremer then tried convincing his captor that he'd gotten the wrong guy. When that didn't work, he tried to negotiate a lucrative business deal if they let him go. The man never gave up complaining, arguing or pleading. Karpis couldn't wait to be rid of him.

But the wait for the ransom turned out to be long and arduous. Endless negotiating with the Bremer family ensued back in St. Paul. Annoyingly, Adolph Bremer tried to slash the ransom for his son down to $100,000. The popular sentiment with the public was to not reward these hoodlums with ransom at all. Folks had grown tired of all the high-profile kidnappings. President Roosevelt even referred to the Bremer kidnapping in one of his

Mr. Chas McGee

You are hereby declared in on a very desperate undertaking. Dont
try to cross us. Your future and B's are the important issue. Follow
These instructions to the letter.
Police have never helped in such a spot and wont this time either.
You better take care of the payoff first and let them do the
detecting later. Because the police usually butt in your friend
isnt none to comfortable now so dont delay the payment.
We demand $200,000.
Payment must be made in 5 and 10 dollar bills--no new money--
no consecutive numbers--large variety of issues.
Place the money in two large suit box catons big enough to hold
the full amount and tie with heavy cord.
No contact will be made until you notify us that you are ready
to pay as we direct.
You place an ad in the Minneapolis Tribune as soon as you have
the money ready. Under personal colum (We are ready Alice)
You will then receive your final instructions. Be prepared to
leave at a minutes notice to make the payoff.

Dont attempt to stall or outsmart us. Dont try to bargain.
Dont plead poverty we know how much they have in their banks.
Dont try to communicate with us we'll do the directing.

Threats arent necessary--you just do your part--we guarantee
to do ours.

Mr. Chas McGee

I have named you as payoff man. You are responsable for my
safety. I am responsable for the full amount of the money.

                    (Signed)   E.C.Bremer

                    Deal only when signature is used.

                    Chas.McGee.Personal.

A transcription of one of the ransom notes from the Bremer kidnapping. *Courtesy of the St. Paul Police Historical Society.*

fireside chats. FBI director J. Edgar Hoover was taking a personal interest in the case, turning up the heat as high as it could go. Every phone call between the gang and the Bremer home was monitored. The gang's pipeline to inside information went away when Tom Brown was removed from the kidnap squad because the feds got suspicious of his actions. To make matters worse, someone called the authorities claiming that Bremer had been killed and buried somewhere in the area, maybe Anoka. With all that blood from his head wound splattered around Bremer's car, the story of his death seemed plausible. Holes were being dug all over the Twin Cities by various groups trying to find the banker's body. The gang had Bremer write letters to his family to assure them that their loved one was indeed still breathing. Freddie, Davis and Ziegler traveled back and forth between Bensenville and St. Paul, picking up the letters, delivering supplies and negotiating with the Bremer family through notes. Stuck in the hideout, Karpis was getting antsy. Will Weaver was about going stir crazy with claustrophobia.

Alvin Karpis endured three excruciatingly long weeks of guarding his grumpy prisoner until the ransom was finally delivered to a prearranged drop-off point just outside Zumbrota, Minnesota. Cracking open the suitcase in Bensenville, the gang found that Adolph Bremer had kindly included a note letting them know he'd been pressured by the FBI into having the money marked, against his wishes. Adolph reasoned in the note that his son should be released anyway as he'd followed through with his end of the bargain. Tired of his argumentative prisoner, Karpis was just fine with that. Bremer was released the next day on February 7, 1934. True to form, he complained

St. Paul police officers standing on the embankment outside Zumbrota Minnesota where the Edward Bremer kidnapping ransom was dropped off. Among the officers is Police Chief Thomas Dahill and Detective Lieutenants Tom Brown and Charles Tierney. *Courtesy of the St. Paul Police Historical Society.*

the entire trip back to Minnesota. The gang had given him a new set of clothing, burning his old ones because Karpis had read that the FBI could lift fingerprints off cloth. Bremer griped about it, mostly unhappy about losing his favorite set of garters. He also grumbled that the cops should have found him in his long twenty-one days of captivity. While Karpis was irked by the constant monologue of complaints, he thought that Bremer had a point with that one.

According to Karpis, Bremer was still grousing when the gang dumped him around the corner from the Rochester train station. Karpis unceremoniously told Bremer to just "beat it!" Karpis sped back to Chicago as fast he could, eager to leave his uncooperative victim behind. Ed Bremer quietly boarded a train back to St. Paul, showing up at his back door to the surprise of his very happy family. Bremer suddenly became less chatty when the FBI began asking him questions. The gang had threatened to kill his little daughter if he talked to the feds. Bremer did eventually give them a detailed description of the wallpaper in the room where he'd been held captive, a tidbit that would eventually be used to convict the gang.

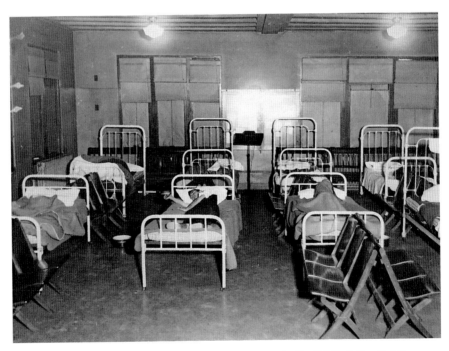

On January 22, 1934, St. Paul police officers slept on cots in the Public Safety Building during the kidnapping of Edward Bremer. *Courtesy of the St. Paul Police Historical Society.*

Back in Chicago, Alvin Karpis wished he'd never heard of Edward Bremer. His feelings that the caper was cursed grew with every passing moment. It was a big payoff, but trying to launder the marked cash would be impossible with the FBI hot to identify the culprits. Karpis felt like the money was "an albatross around my neck." Tensions grew as the search for the kidnappers became the biggest nationwide search since the Lindbergh baby. The members of the gang began fighting among themselves, with Mother Barker stirring the pot more than anyone. Word came in that evidence they had carelessly left behind at the ransom drop was found in Zumbrota.

Completely sick of Chicago, Alvin Karpis and both Barker brothers hit the road to Toledo, Ohio. Alvin brought along his girlfriend, Dolores Delaney, and Freddie had Paula Harmon—"the drunk," as Karpis called her. In Toledo, they met up with several other gang members, including Harry Campbell, Will Weaver, Volney Davis and Edna Murray. While the gang tried to party, tensions were running high. The gang began to bicker even more.

In March, Alvin and Fred went to see Dr. Joseph Moran in Chicago. Doc Moran was always willing to perform a quiet procedure for gangsters like removing a bullet without reporting it or maybe performing an abortion on their moll. Fred and Alvin sought him out for his expertise on removing fingerprints, not wanting to take any chances of being identified in connection with the kidnappings in Minnesota. (And indeed, Wisconsin police would later find some of the gas cans they'd used on the trip to Bensenville and lift fingerprints that the St. Paul kidnap squad would eventually identify as Doc Barker's.) Even though Doc Moran injected their fingertips with cocaine first, the operation turned out to be horribly painful. He scraped at Karpis's fingertips until they were sharpened like pencils. Their hands ached for weeks. Freddie's thumb became horribly infected.

His willingness to undergo that painful procedure illustrates the lengths that Alvin Karpis would go to avoid detection. In fact, at the time, the FBI was still completely unaware of the existence of the Karpis-Barker Gang. Certainly, they all had criminal records—Alvin and Fred were still wanted in Missouri for the murder of the sheriff. But the FBI did not know that Alvin Karpis and Fred Barker had formed a highly efficient gang responsible for many large bank robberies and the two kidnappings in St. Paul. Unaware of the Karpis-Barker Gang, authorities often randomly blamed various gangs for jobs without proof because they wanted to look like they were solving crimes better than they were. Many of the Karpis-Barker Gang's jobs were blamed on others, such as Machine Gun Kelly, Pretty Boy Floyd or, as in the case with the Hamm kidnapping, the Touhy Gang.

THE KARPIS-BARKER GANG MANAGED to escape detection for years for several reasons: Fred and Alvin were always alert and aware, Karpis was very well organized—arguably, better organized than the FBI—and, of course, the protections they received in St. Paul from Tom Brown, Harry Sawyer and Jack Peifer. When asked in later years about being a famous gangster, Alvin Karpis said he didn't seek fame like John Dillinger. Karpis reasoned that celebrity would just make his job harder. It was a lot easier to control his own destiny if he stayed out of the headlines. But by now, underworld snitches had begun to whisper to the feds that the culprits in the Bremer kidnapping were a couple of brothers and an old lady disguised as their mother. Not quite right, but too close for comfort. The Karpis-Barker Gang's name would soon begin to appear in the newspapers as possible suspects.

The FBI learned about the Karpis-Barker Gang when Eddie Green was shot in St. Paul on April 3, 1934. Green had left the gang to join up with John Dillinger and Baby Face Nelson. On March 31, federal agents and St. Paul police raided Dillinger's hideout in the Lincoln Court Apartments on Lexington Avenue. Dillinger escaped, but when searching his abandoned apartment, they found a scribbled telephone number that they traced to one of Green's St. Paul hideouts. When Green and his wife, Bessie, turned up at the house at 778 Rondo, he was ambushed, receiving several Thompson submachine gun bullet wounds to his head and shoulder. Green was taken to Ancker Hospital (today known as Regions Hospital), where he languished in and out of consciousness for seven days. While Green babbled in his delirium, G-men recorded every word he said, which included revealing the existence of the Karpis-Barker Gang. After Green died on April 10, Bessie began to spill information to the police too, confirming that the Karpis-Barker Gang was responsible for the Bremer kidnapping. She even listed the names of all of the gang members along with their girlfriends. Having worked for Harry Sawyer at the Green Lantern, she was quite familiar with them.

Things heated up fast for Alvin Karpis. He began seeing his face on wanted posters, in magazines and movie reels. On July 22, 1934, Alvin and Delores went to see a movie in Cleveland, Ohio, called *Manhattan Melodrama*. They left the theater to hear newsboys announcing the death of John Dillinger, Public Enemy Number One. Dillinger had just emerged from the Biograph Theater in Chicago after watching the exact same movie when he was gunned down by the FBI. Karpis had been good friends with Dillinger. In fact, it was Karpis who had invited Dillinger and Baby Face to come to Minnesota to enjoy the O'Connor System in St. Paul. Hearing about Dillinger's death had to have had some effect on him.

Cuba sounded like a great place to be. Alvin Karpis and Dolores Delaney headed to the Cuban resort town of Varadero. Reality hit home, however, when they heard a radio report on October 22 that Pretty Boy Floyd had been shot and killed. The feds were going after all the heavy hitters. When they killed Baby Face Nelson on November 27, the FBI needed to name a new Public Enemy Number One. J. Edgar Hoover chose Alvin "Creepy" Karpis for the "honor" of being the most wanted man in America. And Karpis didn't like that at all.

In early January 1935, Alvin and Dolores fled Cuba when federal agents showed up after reports that some of the Bremer ransom money had shown up in Havana. They went to Miami, Florida, where they soon met up with Fred Barker. Alvin Karpis was happy to be reunited with his best friend again after all those months. Freddie and Alvin soon took off to Ocklawaha, Florida, where Freddie and his mother were staying in a cabin on Lake Weir. Joining them was Harry Campbell and Wynona Burdette. Campbell had a way of making Karpis laugh. Their current woes seemed to fade for a bit. Freddie and Alvin got back to doing what they enjoyed best: planning a bank robbery.

Meanwhile, Dolores was back in Miami, nesting, pregnant with Alvin Karpis's child for the second time. Alvin had insisted on an abortion the first time, having no particular ambitions on being a father. Children had no place in his chosen life of crime. However, Dolores wanted to keep this baby, and he relented to her wishes. Not that he wanted to get married or anything either—he'd tried that and didn't like it.

ALVIN KARPIS HAD MANY girlfriends. He was attracted to women who were like him: easygoing, lazy, just wanting to have a good time—the kind of woman who suited his lawless and nomadic life. Larry DeVol had introduced him to his first serious lover, Carol Hamilton, back in 1929. She was a prostitute and widow of Freddie's older brother Herman. The thirty-five-year-old Carol was soft on young twenty-one-year-old Alvin because he reminded her of her dead husband. With her skills as a prostitute and her underworld connections, she taught young Alvin many things, in and out of bed. Karpis referred to her as "a fantastic broad." Carol called the skinny Alvin Karpis "Slim"—the same pet name she'd given to her dead husband. For years, he would use her surname as an alias, calling himself

Raymond Hamilton. In fact, Ray was the name most gangsters knew him by. Even Dolores Delaney called him Ray.

In early 1931, Carol introduced Alvin Karpis to Dorothy Slayman, her beautiful, redheaded seventeen-year-old niece. Alvin fell for her immediately, taking her with him on the road. Later that fall, Alvin and Dorothy got married. But the newlyweds didn't enjoy much togetherness. After a quick honeymoon, they drove to Chicago to introduce his new bride to the Karpowicz family. Alvin soon left to meet Freddie to pull some jobs as they were running low on money. He promised Dorothy that he would be home for Christmas; however, he didn't see her again for nearly four years. After Sheriff Kelly was shot during that December 17 robbery in West Plains, Missouri, law enforcement had Dorothy under constant surveillance hoping to find Alvin, even keeping her in jail for a short time in Missouri. He felt bad about Dorothy's troubles but chose to abandon his wife rather than risk capture. Not completely heartless, he wrote her several letters over the years, sending cash for expenses. In the summer of 1935, still feeling sorry about leaving her, Alvin went to visit Dorothy in Oklahoma. Like her aunt, Dorothy was now in the business of running a "massage parlor." He told her she should get a divorce and move on. As her husband was a wanted felon, she would be allowed to obtain a quick divorce for only $1. When she expressed some bitterness, Alvin threw in $500 so she could go to secretarial school. The divorce was finalized a few months later on November 22, 1935.

Alvin Karpis hadn't spent long mourning the split from his wife back in 1931. He met sixteen-year-old Dolores Delaney just a few weeks later, shortly after arriving in Minnesota for the first time. They had met when he paid a visit to the St. Paul home of Pat Reilly, a bartender at the Green Lantern who would later become John Dillinger's wheel man. Dolores was the sister of Reilly's wife, Helen. When Dolores answered his knock at the door, Karpis was immediately taken with the beautiful brown-eyed brunette, calling her "gorgeous." Dolores had been equally smitten when she had first caught sight of Alvin at the Hollyhocks a few days earlier. He would not be her first gangster flame. She had also dated Clarence DeVol, brother of Karpis's buddy Larry DeVol. Choosing to be a gangster moll is not an easy life, with the constant running, hiding, abortions, venereal disease and weeks of abandonment. But none of that mattered to Dolores Delaney when she fell madly in love with Alvin Karpis. After some time, with the help of Harry Sawyer, she ran away from her disapproving family to be free to take up with Alvin. He began escorting her to every speakeasy in the Twin Cities, consorting with the worst elements of the underworld. Eventually, Dolores's mother put her into a Catholic boarding school, hoping to straighten out her wayward daughter. Dolores ran away from the school straight to Harry Sawyer's house to run off with Alvin Karpis.

As fun as it was chumming around with Freddie on Lake Weir, Karpis decided to head back to Miami to check up on Dolores, who, by mid-January 1935, was now eight months pregnant. After finding all was well with his gal, Karpis and Harry Campbell headed off to do some fishing around the Gulf. Alvin Karpis was feeling happy. He and his best friend Freddie had reunited, soon to join forces again on another magnificent Karpis-Barker robbery. He was even getting used to the idea of being a father. When he had left the cottage on Lake Weir, Mother Barker had asked Alvin to let her know when the child arrived. In an uncharacteristic moment of softness toward one of gang's molls, Ma had promised to come down to Miami to help Dolores with the baby while he went off on their jobs. Karpis was pleased with the thought. The future looked good.

Campbell was having such a great time that he chose to hang out fishing for one extra day. When the two got back to Miami a day late, they found Dolores and Wynona sitting in a car parked a block from their house. Dolores was sobbing so hard that Alvin asked her take a breath and tell him what was wrong. He got the shock of his life when Dolores was finally able to speak. Freddie and Ma were dead. His best friend and partner had been shot and killed by the FBI in their cabin at Lake Weir. Campbell would have been dead too if he'd gone back on time. Alvin Karpis was filled with grief. In his book, he referred to Fred Barker as "probably the friend that was closest to me…we never had a falling out, and our names were joined forever in everybody's minds as the leaders of the Karpis-Barker Gang." And now that partnership was suddenly over.

In addition to grief, Alvin Karpis felt fear. If they got Freddie and Ma, he could be next. Dolores and Wynona caught a train to Atlantic City, checking into the Danmore Hotel upon arrival. Karpis and Campbell drove up in their new Buick Special. But Karpis didn't feel safe in Atlantic City either. His sixth sense told him that something was still wrong. When he took Dolores to the doctor for a pregnancy checkup, he couldn't shake the feeling of being followed. He vowed they would leave Atlantic City the next day. But at the break of dawn, the police came pounding on their doors. With Harry Campbell's Tommy gun blazing, the foursome flew past the cops and out the back door. A stray bullet grazed Dolores's leg.

The two gangsters stashed their women in the hotel alley. Alvin promised Dolores he would be right back after they got their car from a nearby garage. They tore out of the garage, with Campbell still firing at the police as they careened out onto the street. During a wild car chase, Karpis used all the skills that earned him the name "Creepy" to evade the cops. When they made it back to the alley, the women were gone—nabbed by the police. After nearly three years together, Alvin Karpis had spent his last night with Dolores Delaney.

Karpis was shacked up in an Ohio whorehouse when he read the news that Dolores had given birth to his son while in custody. She named the baby Raymond Karpowicz in honor of his father's favorite alias. In his 1971 autobiography, Karpis gave the news dispassionately with no comment on how he felt about it. He simply noted that his parents picked up the child and that Dolores and Wynona were sent to Florida to be tried for harboring criminals. But after his arrest in 1936, Alvin sent a heartfelt letter to her from his jail cell in St. Paul: "I don't know how to express my feelings towards you in words, but when I lost you the light just seemed to go out." He ended the letter with some self reflection: "If a person like myself is capable of loving any one or having any affection for another, I certainly feel that way about you."

Dolores Delaney was released from the Florida prison in 1938. She returned to her family in St. Paul, but her son remained in Chicago with Alvin's parents. What happened to her after that has been lost to history. The Delaney and Karpowicz families would never say. Robert Livesey believes that Alvin told her to disappear to avoid a life of being hounded with the notoriety of being the girlfriend of the infamous Alvin Karpis.

While in Toledo, he finally heard the news that Doc Barker and Byron Bolton had been captured in Chicago the week before Freddie and Ma were killed. Everything was changing. Yet Karpis was anxious to pull another job—it had been way too long without a score. But his pool of qualified stick-up men had shrunk considerably. One by one, his peers were being killed or arrested. He was unable to make connections like he did at the Green Lantern in St. Paul. In his book, he dove deeper into the well of self-pity, admitting, "I felt lonely." He decided to rob the payroll from the Youngstown Sheet & Tube in Warren, Ohio, with Harry Campbell. Unfortunately, his friend Fred Hunter, who had suggested the job, was unavailable. Karpis spent a long time scouring for a suitable replacement who lived up to his high professional standards. He finally settled on a morphine addict named Joe Rich. They pulled the job off on April 25,

1935. When the three men ripped open the payroll sacks, Karpis called the $72,000 "a pretty sight." Joe Rich was so excited that he immediately pulled out a needle and shot himself full of morphine. But despite the success, Karpis was feeling off. It just wasn't the same as the good old days because his best friend Freddie Barker wasn't there.

J. EDGAR HOOVER HAD made it his personal mission to find the last major criminal of the gangster era still on the loose, his Public Enemy Number One, Alvin Karpis. But despite the nationwide manhunt for him, Karpis was still itchy for more work. It wasn't the money that drove his desire— he was "aching" for the excitement of pulling off another magnificent heist. And he had the perfect job in mind: a payroll train robbery. He thought it would be thrilling to emulate his old Wild West heroes like Jesse James and the Dalton brothers. Alvin wistfully wished that Fred Barker could have been there for it. This was going to be like the old Karpis-Barker jobs they had spent hours planning in St. Paul—in his words, a "big extravaganza."

Karpis robbed an Erie Railroad mail train at Garrettsville, Ohio, on November 7, 1935, with Harry Campbell, Freddie Hunter and three others. Despite a haul of only $34,000—he had expected at least six times as much—Karpis was still flying high as he drove away on his carefully plotted getaway route. He had finally succeeded in pulling off the Wild West–style train robbery he and Fred Barker had dreamed about.

Alvin Karpis was knocking around the South with Hunter and Campbell when he heard on the car radio that he'd been indicted back in St. Paul for the William Hamm kidnapping. And he also learned that old Charlie Fitzgerald was locked up in Minnesota under indictment for it too.

In the early spring of 1936, the sister of Wynona Burdette, Harry Campbell's old flame, came looking for him, waving a telegram sent from St. Paul. It was from Wynona, asking for $100 to cover her legal expenses in Minnesota. Campbell gave the sister the money to pass along, but Karpis thought something was fishy. Why would Wynona be in Minnesota if she'd just been jailed in Florida for harboring Harry Campbell? It didn't add up. The two quickly left town, and it was a good thing they did. The telegram was indeed a ploy to flush out Campbell and hopefully Karpis as well. Wynona was in St. Paul to testify in the Bremer kidnapping trials of Harry Sawyer and William Weaver. The FBI reasoned that if the money did arrive, it had to be from Campbell, as the Burdette family was flat broke. The feds showed up right after the two gangsters left town. Alvin Karpis's instincts had saved the day again.

There was now a $5,000 reward for information leading to his arrest. He resented the whole manhunt thing. Why couldn't they just leave him alone to do his work? Word came that his Hot Springs apartment had been raided, the raid rumored to have been led by Hoover himself. Karpis was skeptical. He felt that a lot of disinformation was being spread by the FBI director to make himself look good—including a false story that Karpis had sent a letter to Hoover threatening to kill him. Hoover was getting a lot of criticism for randomly shooting up houses but never capturing Karpis. Hoover was even hauled before a Senate appropriations committee to be grilled about his failures. Senator K.D. McKellar of Tennessee pointed out that Hoover couldn't be much of a crime fighter since he'd never personally made an arrest. Karpis reveled in reading about Hoover's troubles.

He rejoined Fred Hunter in New Orleans, Louisiana, to discuss a bank job. But when he reached Fred's apartment, his old anxieties came back. Something again felt terribly wrong. He became suspicious of every car that was behind him; every man sitting on a bench reading a paper made him anxious.

On the morning of May 1, 1936, Alvin Karpis took his car in to be serviced. He was jumpier than ever that day; things didn't feel right. Around 4:50 p.m., he asked Hunter to drive him down to the garage to pick up his car. Looking up and down the street for signs of trouble, Karpis slid behind the wheel of Hunter's car while Fred hopped in the passenger seat. Before Karpis could hit the clutch, a car screeched to a halt in front him. Almost simultaneously, he heard a voice shout through his open window, "Alright, Karpis, just keep your hands on that steering wheel." Dozens of FBI agents materialized out of nowhere, running in with guns loaded and pointing at him. More agents were hanging out of the windows of his apartment building. The G-man holding the gun to his head ordered him to get out of the car. Several agents shouted at him all once, giving orders to sit down while others barked at him to keep standing. Some yelled him to keep his hands up, others snapped at him to keep them down. Hundreds of onlookers came running to see what the commotion was about. It was bedlam. One of the agents called out to a man who had been hanging back in the alley: "We've got him. It's all clear, Chief." As the man walked closer, Alvin Karpis came face to face for the first time with his nemesis, J. Edgar Hoover.

Still stinging from the criticism that he had never actually arrested anyone, Hoover had ordered his men to inform him when Karpis was located so he

Alvin Karpis captured by federal agents and brought back to St. Paul, 1936. *Courtesy of the Minnesota Historical Society.*

could make a big deal of arresting Public Enemy Number One. It irked Karpis that Hoover salvaged his reputation with this arrest claim but had actually just hidden in the shadows until it was safe to come out of hiding. To top it off, no one, including Hoover, had thought to bring handcuffs, so a necktie was tied around Karpis's wrists instead.

He was unhappy to be caught but couldn't help being amused by the chaotic circus. In the car, the G-men, unfamiliar with New Orleans, couldn't find the local FBI office. Smirking, Karpis offered to give them directions.

Three hours after his arrest, he was flown by chartered plane to Minnesota to be tried for the Bremer and Hamm kidnappings. Along with several FBI agents, he was accompanied on the plane by J. Edgar Hoover. There was no way that the beleaguered FBI director was going to miss the photo opportunity of delivering his Public Enemy Number One to justice in St. Paul. And indeed the circus continued. Crowds of onlookers, photographers and reporters gathered at St. Paul's Holman Field to greet the plane. No fewer than thirty FBI agents, many with Tommy guns, surrounded Karpis as he was transferred from the plane to an awaiting car. A short distance away, the crowds and reporters thronged again in Rice Park to watch as the infamous kidnapper was marched into the federal courthouse. Photos of the events in St. Paul were splashed across newspapers coast to coast. Once inside the courthouse, Karpis was led to a third-floor detention room, where he was handcuffed to a radiator. That same radiator is now in a museum in the basement of the old federal courthouse, known today as the Landmark Center.

Hoover started the interrogations by demanding Karpis detail every crime he ever committed. The feds knew about a few Karpis-Barker jobs because the dimwitted Byron Bolton had been squealing like crazy. Karpis didn't mind doing a little bit of bragging about his robberies and such, but he refused to give any useful information. Hoover turned the interrogations over to his agents, ordering them to question their prisoner in shifts, never letting him sleep. For the next four days, a steady stream of FBI agents from all over the country took turns interrogating Karpis around the clock while he sat handcuffed to the radiator, only allowed to use the restroom at night when the public wouldn't see him. Karpis complained that he "felt like an animal." At first, the questioning focused mostly on the Bremer kidnapping. Then they demanded to know who Jack Peifer's connection was within the St. Paul Police Department. How did he always seem to be three steps ahead of them? Who had fed him inside information? Karpis grew weary and groggy after days with no sleep. Still in the clothing he'd been arrested in back in New Orleans, he was filthy and exhausted. Hoover was determined to make him crack. It never happened. Alvin "Creepy" Karpis was no snitch.

On the morning of May 9, Karpis was finally allowed to wash his face and take a nap on a cot that was brought into the detention room. He was given coffee and a small breakfast. That afternoon, an agent informed him that he was to be formally charged by the court clerk. The reason for the respite became clear: Hoover needed his prisoner to look like he'd been treated well. Karpis was handcuffed to Hoover to make a big show of marching his captive thirty feet down the hall past the throngs of reporters and photographers. Karpis was charged with both the Hamm and Bremer kidnappings. His bail was set at a whopping $500,000, the highest criminal bail ever to be set in the United States at that time. Afterward, he was transferred to a real cell at the nearby jail in downtown St. Paul. The FBI did not entrust the guarding of its Public Enemy Number One to the questionable St. Paul police. Federal agents watched him twenty-four hours per day, brought him his food and even cleaned his cell. He was not allowed to read a newspaper or receive any visitors. Karpis was in isolation, but he was never alone. Agents were

Karpis claimed to have been chained to a radiator in the third floor Detention Room on a hot summer day before being brought to the courtroom. He pled guilty soon after.

Alvin Karpis claimed that he was handcuffed to this radiator in the old federal courthouse. It is currently on display in the Landmark Center Museum. *Photo by Bick Smith.*

always within earshot, even when he was meeting with his lawyers. Rumors swirled that some of his pals were planning to bust him out. The FBI agents were heavily armed just in case any gangsters stormed the St. Paul jail. And if they did, the first thing the agents planned to do was shoot Alvin Karpis rather than let him go free.

Karpis pleaded not guilty when brought before the judge in the federal courthouse a few weeks later. Back at the jail, the relentless questioning by federal agents was only interrupted when prosecutors worked on him to change his plea to guilty, promising that if he cooperated, he would receive a light sentence with a chance of early parole. To top it off, Minnesota was experiencing one of its hottest summers on record. The stuffy jail cell didn't help Karpis's mood as he sat waiting for trial, sweating it out literally and figuratively. He was miserable.

Word came on June 8, 1936, that his old partner in crime Larry DeVol had led a mass escape from the psychiatric hospital in St. Peter, taking fifteen criminally insane inmates along with him. One month later, DeVol robbed a bank in Turon, Kansas, and then fled to Enid, Oklahoma, where he and several of his criminally insane buddies went drinking. The bar owner became alarmed at the behavior of the odd group of strangers and called

The detention room in the old federal courthouse. *Photo by Bick Smith.*

the cops. When the police asked DeVol to come along for questioning, he slowly drained his mug, pulled out a gun and fired. Enid police officer Cal Palmer was killed instantly. DeVol ran from the tavern and then jumped on the running board of a moving car. When more cops caught up with him, DeVol was shot nine times, dying in the middle of the street after having killed his sixth police officer.

On July 14, 1936, it was finally time for Alvin Karpis's kidnapping trial. Without fanfare, he changed his plea to guilty. He claimed later that he changed his plea to avoid a long trial in a sweltering courtroom. A long hot summer still lay ahead, and the federal courthouse was not air conditioned. Perhaps Karpis had another reason for his guilty plea. He was still wanted in Missouri, where he faced certain execution for the murder of that sheriff. After a guilty plea, the triumphant Hoover would never give his prize prisoner up to some small-town cops. Kidnapping carried a life sentence, but Karpis wasn't worried about that, as prosecutors had promised him a deal. Two weeks later, he returned to the federal courthouse for his sentencing hearing. But he didn't get the short sentence and early parole as promised. The judge sentenced him to life in prison, with his earliest chance of parole set at fifteen long years away.

THE DAY AFTER HE pleaded guilty to the kidnappings, Alvin Karpis left Minnesota, never to return. Federal agents escorted him to Leavenworth Prison to be processed. On August 7, 1936, he was then sent to the infamous Alcatraz Prison in San Francisco Bay, where he would remain until 1962. His twenty-five years there earned him the record for the longest continuously served time in Alcatraz. Shortly before Alcatraz was closed, Karpis was sent to McNeil Island in Washington State. After a total of thirty-three years in prison, he finally got his parole in 1969. He was released and immediately deported to Canada, his country of birth. His retirement was quite comfortable. The crafty Karpis had planned ahead. Unlike most gangsters, he had entrusted several banks with a large portion of his loot, including a bank in Duluth, Minnesota. Before Social Security numbers, opening an account under a fake name was easy, so the banks were unaware that they had been safekeeping the ill-gotten gains of an infamous gangster. After collecting thirty-three years worth of interest, his stash had grown into a nice little nest egg. His lawyers were able to bring the money to Canada. For a short time, he went into the pizza supply business. He earned more money by writing a book about his criminal career, *Public Enemy Number One: The Alvin Karpis Story*, with Canadian reporter Bill Trent. A production company co-owned by Burt Lancaster paid him a good chunk of change for the rights to produce a movie based on his book. Hollywood heartthrob Steve McQueen was set to play Alvin Karpis. For unknown reasons, the movie was never made.

After a few years, Karpis moved to Costal del Sol, Spain, where the weather was agreeable and his money stretched further. In 1974, he began collaborating with Canadian author Robert Livesey to write his second book, *On the Rock*, about his life in Alcatraz. When Livesey traveled to Spain to meet Alvin Karpis, the elderly gangster was not the hardened criminal he had anticipated. Instead, he found "a pleasant, grand-fatherly individual who was well read and informed." He described Alvin Karpis as a complex person—quiet, funny and practical, with good manners. He was a good storyteller who didn't mind getting a laugh by making fun of himself with tales of his past flubs during robberies that went wrong. People who met him couldn't imagine that he was a killer. Prison psychiatrists had been equally perplexed. They couldn't figure out why the intelligent, thoughtful, logical prisoner sitting before them had become a criminal. During his intake at Leavenworth back in 1936, tests given by psychiatrists determined that he was not the type to be criminally inclined.

In the Canadian documentary, Karpis mused, "Maybe I wasn't all there...maybe I had a mental quirk about these things." But he also asserted that he didn't have the slightest regret about the crimes he'd committed, even when people got killed. He simply stated, "The only thing I was concerned about was us." He mused that perhaps this was a "selfish way of looking at it from the viewpoint of so-called society." But Livesey said that Alvin Karpis didn't really believe he had a mental glitch. And he certainly didn't care what "society" thought of his choices. Karpis felt that what he did was the smart and logical thing to do. He got a kick out of pulling jobs. In his mind, the banks were the bad guys who caused the Depression and then stuck it to poor farmers like his immigrant parents, John and Anna Karpowicz. While most Americans were struggling during the Depression, he was living the high life. He had the money to rent the finest apartments and buy new cars, fancy clothes and diamond rings. When people questioned him at the time how it was that the youthful Karpis had so much money, he would tell them that his father was in the lumber business in Minnesota or a horse salesman in Chicago.

Karpis truly believed that he was better than your ordinary criminal thug. He considered being a bank robber and kidnapper something to be proud of—a profession that took brains and courage. While being interrogated after his capture, Karpis told J. Edgar Hoover, "I'm a thief, I'm no lousy hoodlum." In his book, *On the Rock*, Karpis expressed that despite meeting many friends and associates like Fred Barker and Larry DeVol while incarcerated, he felt that "the majority of the population in any prison is made up of losers from the gutter of society." He wrote that "the worst punishment of any prison is not the confinement, the work, the cruelty of the guards, or the lack of women but the garbage you are forced to live with—your fellow inmates."

AFTER HIS RELEASE, KARPIS had no ambition to return to crime. Not because he thought it would be wrong; rather, he just didn't want to go back to prison. He was enjoying his freedom too much.

However, that didn't stop him from thinking about it. There were two banks where he lived in Spain that he always thought were ripe for a good bank job. He would entertain himself with plotting in his mind how it could be done. Old "Creepy" could retire from bank robberies, but he couldn't retire his mind.

Alvin Karpis died in Spain at age seventy-one on August 29, 1979. The newspapers at first speculated that he committed suicide, as a bottle of sleeping pills was found next to his bed. Livesey, who knew Karpis well, insisted that this could not be true. "Al was not the type of person to give up and take his own life. He was awaiting the publication of the book, but most importantly, he was a survivor, he had survived 33 depressing years in prison." Livesey pointed out that the pill bottle was full and that the Spanish death certificate cited heart attack as the cause of death. Several media outlets immediately retracted the suicide story at the time, but unfortunately, it stuck and is often repeated today.

He was buried at San Miguel Cemetery in Málaga, Spain, under the name Alvin Karpowicz. But it seems his life in hiding did not end with his death. In Spain, you must pay for a long-term lease to remain in your burial plot for more than twenty years. When his grave's lease expired on May 28, 1999, his body was disinterred. No one claimed his remains, so Karpis was reburied in a mass grave somewhere in the mountains—exactly where unknown, impossible to find. America's most successful Public Enemy Number One remains at large even in death.

In his autobiography, Alvin Karpis recalled his time in Minnesota fondly: "But of all the Midwest cities, the one I knew best was St. Paul, and it was a crook's haven. Every criminal of any importance in the 1930s made his home at one time or another in St. Paul. If you were looking for a guy you hadn't seen for a few months, you usually thought of two places—prison or St. Paul. If he wasn't locked up in one, he was probably hanging out in the other. St. Paul was a good spot for both pleasure and business. You could relax in its joints and speakeasies without any fear of arrest, and when you were planning a score, you could have your pick of all the top men at all the top crimes."

Alvin Karpis had lived his life his way, never apologizing for any of it. He considered his years with Freddie Barker as the best ones of his life, both personally and professionally. Whenever anyone asked him if he had any regrets, the former gangster would always smile and give the same response—his only regret was getting caught.

FREDDIE BARKER

Frederick George Barker was born on December 12, 1901, in Aurora, Missouri, and like his older brothers, he appeared with the family on the 1910 census. He was short and slender at five feet, four inches tall and had light-brown hair. He had several gold-capped teeth.

Ironically, his first recorded run-in with the law involved a crime he did not commit. He was detained along with six other people in September 1922 because the car in which he was riding was like a car used by a different gang to commit a bank robbery. He and his friends were questioned and released.

In October, he was arrested, but merely for vagrancy, serving thirty days in jail. On January 6, 1923, he and an accomplice interrupted a poker game, robbing the players at gunpoint. It must have been a high-stakes game, as the total take was around $600. He was arrested a few days later, tried for armed robbery and sentenced to one to five years in the Oklahoma State Reformatory. However, he was paroled after only a short time in prison. Following his release, he teamed up with his brother Herman for several small crimes.

In March 1927, Freddie was sentenced to five to ten years in prison for robbing a bank in Winfield, Kansas. He was sent to Kansas State Prison. Prison did not turn Freddie away from crime, but rather made him a hardened criminal. And it gave him some new friends. He was given a cellmate named Alvin Karpis, who had been transferred from the reformatory in Hutchinson, Kansas. This would prove to be a pivotal

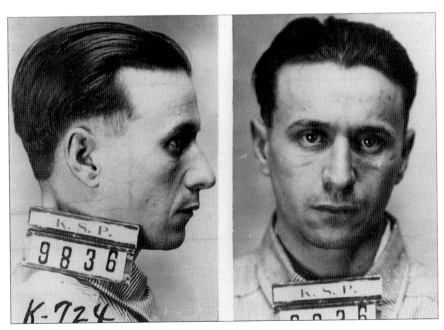

Frederick "Freddie" Barker, Ma Barker's youngest. *Courtesy of the St. Paul Police Historical Society.*

event in Freddie's life. He and Alvin would become friends, indeed almost like brothers, as well as partners in crime.

When Freddie was paroled on March 30, 1931, he made sure that Karpis could find him after his own release. Karpis was released on May 2, 1931. At the time, Ma was living at 401 North Cincinnati Avenue in Tulsa. The house was little more than a tar-paper shack, with no indoor plumbing or electricity. Fred had told Alvin how to find Ma, and the two got together immediately. They began pulling small-time burglaries. There are several unsolved crimes from May 1931 that may have been their doing. The duo was arrested along with four others by the Tulsa police and charged with a jewelry store robbery. Fred's parole was revoked, and he was sent to McAlester Prison to finish his term. Karpis was also reincarcerated, but he was released in September because he arranged to have the stolen jewelry returned.

When Fred was released again, he returned to Tulsa to get Ma and her "man," Art Dunlop. He moved them to a cottage in Thayer, Missouri. Fred probably paid the rent, but it was Dunlop who signed the lease, telling the owner of the cottage that he was a retired oilman. Karpis soon joined them. Dunlop described Karpis as his nephew. Just one big happy family.

They wanted to steal some serious cash. If they were taking risks, they reasoned, they might as well get a big reward. But to pull off big jobs, they needed two things: serious firepower and fast transportation. On September 21, they stole a car from a Chevrolet dealer in Monett, Missouri. Unfortunately, they had not reckoned with the presence of the night watchman, Elisha L. Hagler. Fred fatally shot him as they sped away in their stolen car. From here on out, Alvin and Fred's careers were inseparable, so there is no need for a separate listing of the jobs they pulled. Instead, let us turn to Fred Barker's personality.

Alvin Karpis described Fred extensively in *Public Enemy Number One: The Alvin Karpis Story*. He said that Freddie was "all business" and always handled any situation without emotion. He also says that he could be vicious and was often "free and easy with a gun." "I always had to keep in the back of my mind that my great pal Freddie Barker was a natural killer." Unfortunately, the target of Fred's wrath was often law enforcement. The shooting of Hagler in Missouri was typical of his reaction if a police officer or a security guard got in the way. He had a violent temper and was quick to lash out.

Freddie was a great planner and a perfectionist. He would not tolerate any deviation from the plan for a robbery. If someone didn't follow through as expected, they were not asked to work with the gang again. Karpis said that

Fred would not even let him in on big jobs until he was sure he would trust him to do his part well. He liked to enjoy himself too, although he never let fun interfere with business. He liked going to movies. He loved the outdoors and was a good swimmer and an avid fisherman. Karpis said, "Freddie was a great companion and a guy who liked to laugh."

He was popular with the ladies, although not particularly handsome, and he had a lot of personal charm. He certainly enjoyed female companionship. Karpis said that girls liked Freddie, enjoying the good time he could show them, as well as the money he had to spend. He was probably most serious with Paula Harmon, widow of bank robber Charlie Harmon. He went so far as to arrange to have her meet Ma while Ma was living at the Commodore Hotel in St. Paul in 1933. Apparently, the meeting did not go well. Paula later told the FBI, "Evidently, I did not make a favorable impression, as I have never seen her since." Freddie was always Ma's favorite son, and their relationship was very close. It is possible that Ma deliberately drove a wedge between Freddie and any girl.

Freddie lived with Paula at 204 Vernon Avenue during May and June 1933, while the Hamm kidnapping was being planned and carried out. They told the homeowners that they were Mr. and Mrs. J. Stanley Smith and that Freddie was a salesman. Later, the couple rented an apartment at the corner of Dale Street and Grand Avenue, under the name of Mr. and Mrs. Edwin Bergstrom. It was there that much of the planning of the kidnapping of Edward Bremer was done. Paula would sit in the kitchen with Wynona Burdette and drink beer. The women did their best to ignore what was happening in the living room.

Freddie's ruthlessness could manifest in ways that weren't violent. With a bunch of newspapers describing some of the gang's activities spread out, Freddie caught Jess Doyle as he was bragging to a few girls about his exploits. Freddie immediately told Doyle that he was a liability that the gang did not want around and refused to work with him ever again. Karpis later said that the only thing that saved Doyle's life that day was that Freddie thought of him as a friend.

Someone who wasn't a friend would not be so lucky. Joseph Moran was a medical doctor who had a thriving medical practice in his early years. Problems with alcohol caused him to lose business, so he turned to illegal operations to make a living. He was sent to prison in 1928 for performing abortions. He was so good at running the prison hospital that he was paroled early and his medical license restored. But alcohol got the better of him again, and he resorted to being a doctor to gangsters, including the Dillinger

Dale Apartments in 2019. Fred Barker rented an apartment here in December 1933 and January 1934. The gang met in this apartment to plan the Bremer kidnapping. *Photo by Craig Frethem.*

Gang and the Karpis-Barker Gang. In the spring of 1934, he performed surgery to obscure the fingerprints of both Karpis and Freddie Barker. He was unable to keep his mouth shut about it, especially when he had been drinking. He vanished in July 1934. Freddie later told Karpis that he and Doc "shot the son of a bitch."

On November 8, 1931, Alvin and Freddie went to Pocahontas, Arkansas, to check out a bank they thought would be a good target for a robbery. Unfortunately, Albert Manley Jackson, a night marshal, observed them watching the bank and became suspicious. He was in the process of writing down their license number when Freddie spotted him. Freddie forced Jackson into their car at gunpoint, and then they drove out of town to a quarry, where Freddie ordered him to get out and start walking. Freddie shot him four times in the back. Another man confessed to the killing and was sentenced to life in prison, but Karpis confirmed that Freddie was the actual murderer when he wrote his autobiography. He said it was typical of Freddie. The man had their license plate number— he had to be silenced, and Freddie wasn't going to hesitate to do what he thought had to be done.

In December 1931, Freddie once again proved that he needed little provocation to shoot. Karpis had been checking out a bank in West Plains, Missouri, for a possible robbery. While there, he noticed a nearby men's clothing store, C.C. McCallon's. He must have liked what he saw in the display window because on the night of December 17, he and Fred removed two bars from a window in the rear of the store, entered and helped themselves to more than $2,000 in merchandise. The local newspaper pointed out that thieves had been very discriminating in what they stole. They didn't just go in and grab a lot of stuff, but "[t]ies, gloves, sweaters and shirts…were selected carefully as to quality and the latest styles."

On the nineteenth, Karpis and Fred drove into West Plains again, picking up a hitchhiker named Robert Gross along the way. They visited Davidson's Auto Shop to get tires repaired. The proprietor noticed articles of clothing in the car that matched the description of the items stolen from McCallon's. He called Mr. McCallon, telling him about his suspicions and asking if he wanted to come over to see if he could identify his property. Then Davidson saw the sheriff, Roy Kelly coming out of the post office across the street. Davidson alerted Kelly, who went to his car to get a pistol. He found McCallon waiting outside the garage, and the two men entered together. Kelley walked up to the passenger side of the car with the intention of talking to Fred. But he never got a word in. Fred shot him in the chest at point-blank range and twice in his left arm. Fred quickly moved over to the driver's side of the car and took off. Kelley died at the scene.

Karpis managed to escape from the scene by running down an alley. He lost his jaunty, stolen red scarf in the process. In a sad side note, the townsfolk had seen Robert Gross come into town with the pair of criminals, and they set upon him immediately. He suffered a severe beating before he could convince people that he had simply hitched a ride from the wrong people at the wrong time.

In his biography, Karpis claimed that he was not there that day, and it was William Weaver who drove the car; however, eyewitness accounts place him on the scene. The official wanted poster issued for the murder of Sheriff Kelley shows mug shots of both Karpis and Fred Barker and a reward of $1,200. The bank was never robbed. After the murder of the sheriff, authorities located the gang's hideout. The gang had left in haste. There was much left behind, including photos, letters and about half of the stolen finery from C.C. McCallon's.

Perhaps most disturbing of all these incidents is what happened near Como Park in St. Paul on the afternoon of Friday, December 16, 1932.

The gang had just robbed the Third Northwestern National Bank in Minneapolis. It had not gone smoothly, and one police officer was already dead, with another mortally wounded. One of the tires of their getaway car had been shot during the melee, and the gang had been driving on a flat tire at breakneck speed down icy roads along "Bank Robbers Row," a common escape route from Minneapolis back to St. Paul.

They had hidden a second car just over the border between the two cities. By the time they reached this backup automobile, their original car was so badly disabled that they had to grab the loot and jump into the second vehicle. Unfortunately, they had obtained this car by stealing it, and it still had "hot" license plates. There were new plates inside the car, and they decided to take the time to make the change. While this was going on, another car pulled up. The car was being driven by twenty-nine-year-old Oscar Erickson, and the passenger was his friend Arthur Zackman. They were out trying to make a little extra money for the holidays by selling Christmas wreaths. When they came upon the gangsters changing the license plates, they slowed down.

Freddie told them, "Get going. Or else." Apparently, they did not move fast enough, as Fred shot Erickson in the head. Zackman leaned over and took over the wheel, and they got out of there as quickly as possible, driving to the nearest police station at University Avenue and St. Alban's. The St. Paul police, seeing the man covered in blood and excitedly blathering on about bullet holes in his car, mistakenly thought that Zackman was one of the robbers from the Third Northwestern Bank. They roughed the poor man up a bit before figuring out he was an innocent civilian. Erickson died in the hospital the next day from his wounds, leaving behind a young widow he had married just two years before.

Freddie Barker was full of contradictions: a loyal friend, a charming lady's man and a vicious and cold-blooded killer. He never stood trial for any of his crimes, dying in a gun battle with the FBI.

ARTHUR "DOC" BARKER

Arrie Barker's third son was Arthur, known as Doc. He was born on January 4, 1899. He filled out a draft card for World War I on September 12, 1918. He stated that he was a native-born citizen of the United States and that his occupation was "in prison"; he listed his employer as the Tulsa County Jail. Describing himself as of medium height and build with gray eyes and brown hair, he indicated that his next of kin was his father, George. Karpis described Doc as short and stocky with a mustache and slicked-back hair. He also said he "didn't look dangerous," but he had an "itchy trigger finger." On the 1920 federal census, he was listed as an inmate of the Tulsa County Jail.

Doc was released from his life sentence in Oklahoma on September 10, 1932, on the condition that he would never return to Oklahoma. He had served only thirteen years. His brother Freddie and Alvin Karis bribed some prison officials to secure such an early release. He joined the Karpis-Barker Gang in Minnesota, but he was not a leader. Doc was a follower, and he did whatever Freddie and Alvin suggested.

His exploits with the Karpis-Barker Gang have already been discussed, but he was different from his brothers in several ways. There are two personality traits often associated with Doc Barker. The first is that he was not too bright. Evidence of that can be found in Doc's letter to his brother Freddie just before the Florida shootout. The letter is filled with poor grammar and inaccurate punctuation. However, this may show poor education rather than low intelligence. Years later, a fellow inmate in Alcatraz would describe Doc as "cunning."

The other trait is a violent temper. The first example is the shooting of Officer Leo Pavlak in South St. Paul. The robbery of the Swift Company payroll, more than $30,000, was covered the next day in newspapers all over the country. Eyewitnesses reported that Doc, armed with a sawed-off shotgun, ordered the officer to "Stick 'em up." Even though the officer complied, he shot him at point-blank range, nearly blowing his head off, and calling him a "dirty rat, son of a bitch."

The second example was the beating he gave Edward Bremer at the time of the kidnapping. As Bremer stopped at the stop sign on Lexington, Volney Davis approached the driver's side window. Showing a pistol, he ordered Bremer to move over. Doc opened the passenger door and, apparently angered by the banker's resistance, reached over to strike Bremer on the head several times with the butt end of a revolver. Head wounds bleed profusely, and so much blood was splashed around the interior of the car that when it was found later in the day, police thought they might be investigating a murder rather than a kidnapping. Doc also placed a pair of goggles covered with tape onto Bremer's face as a blindfold. Doc threatened Bremer with retribution if he should ever identify or testify against the gang. "I have plenty of contacts out there who would get you." Bremer would later say that he was terrified during the trial in the spring of 1935 because of Doc's threats. During his entire testimony, he never looked at Doc.

Above: Police photo taken of the South St. Paul Post Office where the Karpis-Barker Gang pulled off the Swift payroll robbery. *Courtesy of the St. Paul Police Historical Society.*

Right: The goggles used to blindfold Edward Bremer during the kidnapping. *Courtesy of the St. Paul Police Historical Society.*

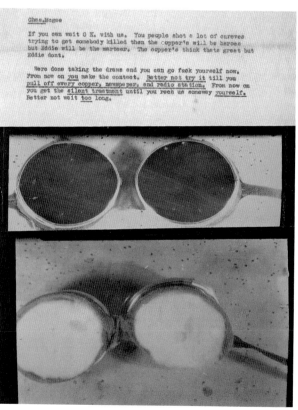

Doc demonstrated his violent streak again in 1935 when he dealt with William J. Harrison, a gang member who had become too talkative. Doc convinced his victim to meet him in a barn just north of Chicago, shot him with a Tommy gun, dismembered the corpse and set fire to the barn. Doc let Freddie know that the deed had been done in a letter a few days later. "I am just Standard Oil," he bragged, "always at your service Ha-Ha!"

Doc could also be frightening, even to his associates. When Wynona Burdette, girlfriend of one of the other gang members, was called on to testify against him in his 1935 trial for the kidnapping of Edward Bremer, the *Minneapolis Star* reported that she "appeared terrified" under the gaze of Doc's "penetrating eyes" and that she spoke so timidly that the judge had to constantly remind her to speak up.

Doc did not have girlfriends like the rest of the group. Gladys Sawyer said that she never saw Doc with a girl, and she wondered if all the time that he spent in prison might have caused him to no longer like the company of women. That changed just before his capture when he became involved with twenty-six-year-old Mildred Kuhlman. She was a striking brunette with short curly hair, an oval face and a rather sharp nose and chin. When testifying at the Bremer kidnapping trial, she painted a very different picture of Doc Barker. She said she ran into Doc on the street in Toledo in June 1934. She told him that an ex-boyfriend was pursuing her with an icepick, intent on killing her. Doc arranged for her to go with him to Chicago, where she did not have to live in fear. "He took care of me and was always kind," she said. "He was one of the best friends I ever had in my life." She admitted that she knew he had to be "some kind of criminal," but she claimed ignorance of the extent of his lawlessness.

Melvin Purvis gave an extensive description of the capture of Doc Barker in the article he wrote for the *Oklahoman* newspaper, published on December 6, 1936. He said that the bureau knew that Doc was in Chicago but could not locate him. They had spotted two known female associates of the gang in downtown locations. One of those women was Mildred Kuhlman. The FBI decided to shadow the women in the hope that they would lead them to the hideout. To avoid discovery, the FBI used several different agents so no one person would stand out as following the women.

Purvis admitted to being surprised when this technique worked. The girls eventually led them to two different apartments on Chicago's North Side, the Pine Grove Apartments and the Surf Lane Apartments. Agent E.J. Connelley, who would later lead the task force that killed Freddie and Ma Barker, was in charge of the raid. On January 8, 1935, he and several

WANT $50,000? JUST BRING THEM IN

John Dillinger $10,000

"Baby Face" Nelson $10,000

Alvin Karper $5,000

Arthur Barker $5,000*

Homer Van Meter $5,000

"Pretty Boy" Floyd $5,000

The wanted posters of Alvin Karpis and Arthur "Doc" Barker, with other infamous gangsters John Dillinger, Baby Face Nelson, Homer Van Meter and Pretty Boy Floyd. The newspaper spelled Karpis's name wrong. *From the collection of Pam Paden Tippet.*

other agents began surveillance of the Pine Grove apartment early in the evening, but it appeared that no one was home and there were no lights on. Nevertheless, they surrounded the building and continued to watch. They were on the verge of giving up when they saw one man go inside the rear of the building and a light go on in the apartment. Shortly after that, a man and two women went in the front entrance.

Connelley went into the building and discovered an intercom system with a call button for each apartment. He rang the buzzer and was rewarded by a woman's voice answering him. He inquired if Mr. Bolton was in. When the woman replied that Mr. Bolton was not at home, Connelley decided that it was time to act. He told her that he was a federal agent and that the apartment building was surrounded—there was no possibility of escape. He told her if everyone came downstairs with their hands up, there would be no violence. At first, there was no response, so he repeated the same message a few minutes later.

Finally, a woman came down carrying a small dog. She identified herself as Clara Gibson. Then a man came down the stairs. Connelley recognized him immediately as Byron Bolton.

At that same time, shots rang out from behind the apartment building. Russell Gibson, aka Slim Gray, had tried to evade capture by climbing out one of the windows. He was armed with a Browning automatic rifle and a .32-caliber pistol. But there were a dozen agents waiting in the rear, and he was shot. One of the agents asked him if he was Alvin Karpis. Gibson gave them his name but refused to say anything more about the gang, even though he was pressed by the agents for the whereabouts of Doc Barker. He died in the hospital. According to G-men, his last words were "Tell you nothing."

A very successful raid, but it was the stakeout at the Surf Lane Apartments that yielded the big fish. Two of Conelley's handpicked agents, Jerry Campbell and Alexander Muzzy, were watching the place from a parked automobile. Two people stepped out the front door: Mildred Kuhlman and Doc Barker. The two agents left their car, and Campbell slipped a Thompson submachine gun under his coat as they followed the couple for a short distance. Doc must have been suspicious because he kept glancing over his shoulder. During one of those backward glances, Campbell pulled out the machine gun. Muzzy took out his pistol, identified himself as a federal agent and ordered Doc to surrender. Other agents who had been standing by stepped out of the shadows, and Doc and Mildred found themselves surrounded.

Doc pretended to raise his hands but quickly took off, darting between two parked vehicles. His escape was short-lived, as he slipped on some ice and fell. Campbell handcuffed Doc and placed him in a waiting FBI car. According to G-men, one of the agents asked Doc where his gun was, and he replied, "Home and ain't that a hell of a place for it."

The agents searched Doc's apartment and found a cache of weapons that included a Thompson submachine gun. Ballistics conclusively linked the weapon to the shooting of Officer Miles Cunningham in Illinois and also proved that it was the same gun stolen from the South St. Paul police car during the robbery of the South St. Paul Post Office in August 1933, thus adding to the evidence that that crime had been carried out by the Karpis-Barker Gang.

Landmark Center in 2019. Built as the Federal Building in 1902, it housed the courtrooms where Doc Barker and Alvin Karpis received their sentences. *Photo by Craig Frethem.*

Word of Doc Barkers's arrest was kept quiet from the public and the press. The FBI didn't want the other members of the gang to get nervous and go deeper into hiding.

Doc was sent to St. Paul to stand trial for the kidnapping of Edward Bremer. The trial began in the spring of 1935. Doc never took the stand in his own defense and was found guilty on May 17. Federal judge M.M. Joyce handed down a life sentence, saying, "Arthur Barker you have no defense in this case. No one could doubt your guilt." Doc showed no emotion.

After being processed at Leavenworth, he was sent to Alcatraz, where he had a reputation as one of the worst troublemakers. He and Alvin Karpis worked together in the prison shop.

Friday, January 13, 1939, turned out to be a very unlucky day for Doc Barker. During a bed check, at around 4:00 a.m., guards discovered that he and four other inmates were not in their cells. All the men were desperate criminals, serving life terms for kidnapping and bank robbery. They had sawed through the bars of their cells and climbed out a window, dropping about ten feet to the ground. Authorities would later say that they had no idea how the men got the saws. There was a heavy fog that night, and the men were not found until they were nearly at the edge of San Francisco Bay, apparently planning to swim to freedom, an attempt that they were unlikely to survive. The guards ordered the men to stop, but they refused and continued to run toward the water. The guards had no choice but to open fire. Two of the five were wounded, at which point they all surrendered. Doc was shot in the head and left leg. He lived for the rest of that day but died in the prison hospital on the fourteenth.

Doc is buried in a potter's field in Olivet Memorial Park in California. There is a small marker in the plot in Oklahoma where the rest of the family is buried. It reads in part, "Lord, I deserve justice, but mercy is what I plead." This may be particularly true for Doc Barker.

EDNA MURRAY

Making a living as a 1930s gangster was pretty much a man's job. Bonnie Parker of the infamous duo Bonnie and Clyde may arguably be the only woman to attain that "honor." Edna Murray, the "Kissing Bandit," came close. Though not a full-fledged member of the Karpis-Barker Gang, she was much more than your ordinary gun moll. In the end, Edna would express that her two favorite cities during her time running with the gang had been Reno, Nevada, and St. Paul, Minnesota. While Reno was fun, St. Paul was the place where gangsters could relax and party without fear, thanks to the O'Connor Layover System.

Martha Edna Stanley was born on May 26, 1898, near Marion, Kansas. She was the fourth of six children, but as the firstborn daughter and pretty cute from the start, she was quite spoiled by her adoring father. Growing up in Cardin, Oklahoma, she learned at an early age how to wrap the opposite gender around her fingers.

As an adult, Edna built on the manipulative ways she had learned as a daddy's girl. She liked to think of herself as "all that." One of her arrest cards described her as five feet and one and a half inches tall, 115 pounds with

Martha Edna Stanley, better known as Edna Murray, Kissing Bandit. *From the collection of Pam Paden Tippet.*

light auburn hair and dark-blue eyes. Bess Green, wife of gangster Eddie Green, described Edna to the FBI in less flattering terms, saying that she was "small through the back and built like a tent," with a mouth full of gold teeth. Either way, Edna used her looks and her sexuality to get what she wanted, never lacking for male companionship.

Edna's flirtatious ways landed her an unplanned pregnancy when she was seventeen years old. She married the baby's father, George Paden, but they most likely never lived together very long, if at all. Edna's son, Preston Paden, the only child she would ever bear, was born on December 27, 1915. Her divorce was finalized one year later. Never one to be without a man for long, she immediately married a shady character named Walter Price, but that ended quickly too, probably because Edna preferred to drink and party more than being a wife and mother.

When Prohibition went into effect on January 17, 1920, Edna was twenty-one years old, twice divorced and saddled with a four-and-a-half-year-old kid. Unable to find work near her parent's home in Cardin, she moved in 1921 to Sapulpa, Oklahoma, where she found a job as a waitress at the Imperial Café. Her entrance into the world of criminals and the Karpis-Barker Gang came when a tall, handsome, dark-haired stranger strolled into the restaurant. Edna was immediately smitten. He introduced himself as "Freddie Jackson." In reality, he was Volney Davis of the Central Park Gang in Tulsa, Oklahoma, which had included his childhood friends, the infamous Barker brothers. Edna was twenty-three years old, and Volney was just nineteen. She claimed to be unaware that he was a gangster until after she had fallen deeply in love. She called him "Curly" Jackson because of his thick, wavy hair. She called him that for the rest of their time together, even after learning his real name. His daring, devil-may-care demeanor was perfect for the wild, young Edna. Volney "Curly" Davis would remain her sweetheart on and off for the next fourteen years until the Karpis-Barker Gang began to unravel in 1935. The breaks in their togetherness were mostly due to one or the other being tossed in jail.

Volney was sentenced to life in prison in early 1923 for a robbery that resulted in the death of a night watchman. Edna visited him in prison a few times and always sent him gifts for Christmas. Even though "Curly" was her true love, she wasn't the type to be without a man and the benefits thereof for very long. She soon took up with "Diamond Joe" Sullivan, recently paroled from Leavenworth after serving time for grand larceny. After only two months of romance, Edna claimed to have married Joe in Los Angeles. There may have actually been a wedding, but it would also be in her nature to not worry about those pesky little legalities. Either way, it didn't last long. He was quickly arrested and convicted of murdering two police officers in Little Rock, Arkansas. Edna was now heading off to prison to visit both her lover, Volney, and her husband, Diamond Joe. When Sullivan was convicted, Edna took part of the cash her mother-in-law had sent to go toward her son's legal defense and headed to Kansas City, Missouri, where she rented an eight-room flat. She supported herself by renting out her extra rooms. She had filled them with nice furniture, paid for again with her husband's defense fund. She also had a nice side business bootlegging alcohol.

As always, Edna could not be alone for long. While her husband was sitting on death row, she started dating another hoodlum named Jack Murray. She suspected that this was not his real name, but she'd learned not to pry into the pasts of men she hooked up with. Jack had just been released from Leavenworth, where he'd been serving time for trafficking in prostitution. Edna and her younger sister Doris Stanley, who also had a penchant for dating criminals, soon moved into Murray's apartment. On April 18, 1924, Diamond Joe Sullivan was executed by electric chair. With her husband dead and her lover serving a life sentence, Edna was free to marry Jack Murray. Again, it is unknown whether a legal marriage actually took place, but she began to refer to herself as Edna Murray.

Settled into a comfortable life bootlegging with Jack, Edna was surprised to open the morning paper on January 9, 1925, to read that Volney Davis had escaped from the Oklahoma penitentiary. When Volney showed up at her apartment, Edna found herself in the odd situation of living under the same roof simultaneously with her fourth husband and her escapee lover. She and her beloved "Curly" had a fun time reuniting, moving into one of the spare bedrooms down the hall. What her husband, Jack, thought of this is unknown. It's very possible he didn't really notice, as he was often heavily under the influence of morphine and hooch. But Edna and Volney were not destined to be happy together for long. About a week later, the apartment was raided by cops looking for illegal alcohol. Volney was quickly returned to the Oklahoma pen.

With Jack Murray, Edna not only bootlegged but also graduated to doing robberies. One time, they broke into a house, where she stole a beautiful long string of pearls from a safe. She was quite proud of that one, wearing the pilfered pearls often. In later years, she promised her only grandchild, Pam, that the pearls would someday be passed on to her. (They weren't.)

The Murrays were arrested several times after being raided for selling alcohol but were never prosecuted until they committed the robbery that earned Edna her famous moniker "Kissing Bandit." In early April 1925, the authorities confiscated twenty cases of their alcohol coming up from New Orleans. With their product gone, Jack and Edna were suddenly broke, so they turned to highway robbery. They chose a certain minister as their target because he had a side job as a courier, delivering cash to the bank for local businesses. They knew that his pockets would be full. They forced the minister into their car at gunpoint. Edna was seemingly having a good old time with it, brazenly waving at traffic cops as they drove through town with their victim. At one point, she even sweetly asked a policeman for directions. When they reached an isolated area out in the country, they relieved the minister of $112 cash and $83 in checks. They took his shoes so he would have a hard time walking quickly back to town, giving them time to escape before the crime was reported. The minister, none too pleased, heatedly gave them a good piece of his mind. Always confident in her good looks and sexuality, Edna laughingly offered to give the furious preacher a kiss as compensation. He turned her down. She was most likely not pleased, as she was unable to fathom how anyone could resist her charms.

By now, Edna Murray was well known to the Kansas City police as an associate of thieves and bootleggers. When it was reported that the bandits were a man and a woman, she was hauled in for a lineup. Witnesses not only

KISSING BANDIT WON TITLE WITH OFFERS—NOT KISSES

ST. PAUL, March 6—(Æ)—Edna Murray, held on federal charges of complicity in the kidnaping of Edward G. Bremer, won her sobriquet of Kansas City's "kissing bandit" without giving her victims a single kiss.

Widow of "Diamond Joe" Sullivan, who was electrocuted in 1924 at Little Rock, Ark., for the murder of a prison guard, the blonde-haired Edna was accused of a hotel holdup and the robbery of a clergyman in Kansas City in 1925.

Offer Refused

She drove the motorcar in which the minister, the Rev. H. H. Southard was kidnaped and robbed of his valuables and his shoes. When the holdup was over, Mrs. Murray offered to kiss the victim goodbye, but he declined. Identifying her later in the police "showup," he still declined.

Mrs. Murray was convicted of first degree robbery and sentenced to 25 years in the Missouri penitentiary, from which he escaped in 1931. Her recent arrest near Pittsburg, Kas., when Jess Doyle, fugitive in the Bremer case, also was trapped, followed investigation of a shooting on a Kansas City street in which Vinita Stacey, Edna's sister, was held.

"All my life I've been a good girl," said Edna, following her most recent detention. "All my life I've been a victim of circumstances."

Loved Fugitive

She admitted, however, a love dating back some 14 years for Fordney Davis, another Bremer

EDNA MURRAY

case fugitive, who escaped from a federal agent at Yorkville, Ill., about the time Edna was apprehended in Kansas. Officers working on the case believed the gang of suspects broke up and scattered from Kansas City after Mrs. Stacey's arrest.

In recent years Mrs. Murray said she had lived in many parts of the country, keeping house for Davis, who worked at odd jobs and "made an honest living in gambling games."

Edna Murray often made the news. This *Miami News* clipping explains how she gained the name "Kissing Bandit." *From the collection of Pam Paden Tippet.*

identified her as the woman who robbed the minister but also asserted that she seemed to be the one who was in charge. Edna acted like she was the victim, throwing several loud tantrums while in jail. After being sentenced to twenty-five years to life at her October 1, 1925 trial, she was dragged out of court screaming, "I've been framed!"

When the story of her playful offer to kiss the preacher came to light during the trial, the Kansas City newspapers dubbed her the "Kissing Bandit." She was also called "the Flapper Bandit" due to her good looks and fashionable attire. In later years, the legend grew that Edna gave out kisses to all her victims, but she asserted that it was just the one time.

Edna was remanded to the Missouri State Penitentiary, where she only stayed a year and a half before making her first escape from prison on May 2, 1927. Her freedom lasted four years. She was recaptured in Chicago on September 10, 1931. She was physically in pretty bad shape—sickly, thin and in withdrawal. Drugs, booze and a life on the lam had taken their toll. But two months later, she had recovered enough to escape again. On November 11, 1931, Edna and two other convicts jumped the fence. All three women were captured the next day when bloodhounds tracked them down. Her third escape came a year later on December 13, 1932. Edna and another woman sawed through bars with hacksaw blades that they had somehow managed to get smuggled inside. For the rest of her life, the normally loquacious Edna refused to divulge who provided the saws.

As the only person to have ever successfully escaped from the Missouri Penitentiary three times, the newspapers gave Edna Murray another name: "Triple Escape Queen." She took pride in that one. When she joined up with the Karpis-Barker Gang, the guys called her "Rabbit" because they admired her ability to "jump out of the hole"—the hole being prison.

Volney "Curly" Davis had been released on a temporary leave of absence from prison one month before Edna's latest escape. Her sister Doris brought Edna a letter from Doc Barker relating the happy news, and soon the lovers reunited in Missouri. Accompanying Volney were Doc Barker and Jess Doyle. Doris was immediately smitten with Doyle. The group then headed to Chicago to meet up with Fred Barker and the rest of the gang. Edna and Volney started partying heavily with the Barker brothers and their new friend, Alvin "Creepy" Karpis. Other members of the gang she met there included Frank "Jelly" Nash, Verne Miller, Earl Christman and Eddie Green. It was also here that she was introduced to Kate Barker. Mother Barker didn't like the women who hung around with her boys. Ma disliked Edna at first sight, and Edna returned the sentiment. Right from the start, she also had problems with Freddie's girlfriend, Paula Harmon. Paula, a drunk and drug addict herself, never missed a chance to inform Edna of Volney's unfaithfulness with other women. Paula would often accuse Edna and Volney of being hangers-on, running with the gang just to live off Freddie's hard-earned stolen loot.

IN EARLY APRIL 1933, Volney and several Karpis-Barker Gang members took a mysterious trip out of town. Upon his return, he nonchalantly mentioned that Earl Christman wouldn't be around anymore. Earl had been shot and killed during a bank robbery in Nebraska. Christman's death did nothing to slow down the partying. In fact, things got even wilder because they now had money to burn from the bank heist. Edna later explained: "Outlaws didn't save up for a rainy day, they bought their fun—and lot's of it—while they still could." She was happy to be in the middle of it.

On June 15, 1933, the Karpis-Barker Gang kidnapped brewery president William Hamm Jr. in St. Paul. At the time, Edna was in Chicago, while Volney was visiting family in Missouri. They were both happy to have an alibi, as the brazen kidnapping generated a lot of heat with national headlines.

Volney returned to Chicago a few days after the kidnapping to hear that Verne Miller and Pretty Boy Floyd had gone to Kansas City to free their cohort Frank "Jelly" Nash, who was in custody and on his way to Leavenworth. The June 17, 1933 caper was a fiasco, involving the deaths of Nash, three cops and a federal agent. Two days later, Miller showed up at Edna's apartment. While Volney stashed Miller's car in their garage, Edna ordered her son, Preston, who was visiting from Oklahoma, to go live with his Aunt Doris for awhile. No way Edna wanted her seventeen-year-old boy in the apartment if the feds stormed it looking for the "Kansas City Massacre" murderer. Miller was panicky. As a former police officer himself, he knew what happened to cop killers. And he was responsible for the deaths of four. After a few days, Miller fled to the East Coast, which he hoped would be a safer place to hide.

Afterward, Edna's son went back to Oklahoma. Her sister Doris and her sweetheart, Jess Doyle, went to Minnesota to go fishing. Edna became worried when she heard no word from them for weeks. Unfortunately, Doris had failed to mention exactly where they had planned to go angling. With more than ten thousand lakes in Minnesota, the options were hard to narrow down. Edna decided that she needed to go there herself to track them down. September 1933 found her traveling to Minnesota for the first time. Edna and Volney went straight to the Green Lantern speakeasy in St. Paul. Under the O'Connor System, gangsters checked in at the Green Lantern with proprietor Harry Sawyer, who kept a running list on the whereabouts of all the gangsters in the Twin Cities. Plus Sawyer was pretty tight with the Karpis-Barker Gang. Therefore, Sawyer seemed like a good place to start. But Sawyer claimed to have no idea as to the whereabouts of Doris and Jess. She would find out much later that Sawyer was less than truthful. He did indeed know where they were, but Sawyer had had a falling out with Doyle and didn't really feel like helping out him or any of his friends. As a powerful figure in the St. Paul underworld, with the local police securely in his back pocket, he wouldn't have seen the need to aid anyone who had offended him.

Disappointed, Edna stayed in St. Paul a few days trying to figure out what to do next. Minnesota was a big state, much of it rural. If the great fixer Harry Sawyer was unable to help, she had no idea how to find Doris on her own. She finally left Minnesota to visit her brother Harry Stanley and his wife, Sybil, in Pittsburg, Kansas. Upon arrival, she got more bad news. Her brother was off in Oklahoma attending the funeral of their father. Being on the run, Edna had been unaware of her beloved father's death. Much later, she discovered that her sister Doris had also attended the funeral. Doris and Jess had not been in Minnesota at the time after all. Doris had learned of their father's death while fishing with Jess in Three Lakes Township, a very remote area of southwestern Minnesota near Redwood Falls. Edna was furious that Doris had not let her know about their father's passing. Not that she could have attended the funeral anyway, what with being a wanted three-time escapee. Afterward, Doris and Jess went straight back to Minnesota for more fishing, bypassing the angry Edna waiting for them in Kansas.

Things got even worse when she returned to Chicago. A huge fight with Volney over his many infidelities with other women resulted in Edna packing her bags and taking off alone. She headed back to Minnesota once more to try to locate her sister. When she arrived, Edna was delighted to find that Doris and Jess were living in an apartment in south Minneapolis. With all apparently forgiven regarding the funeral, she moved in with Doris to try to figure out what to do next. The Twin Cities had a thriving speakeasy community, so this seemed like a nice place for a party-loving gal like Edna to settle in for a while. A few days later, Volney came running to Minnesota to beg for her forgiveness. Of course, she took her "Curly" back. Volney and Edna rented an apartment of their own in south Minneapolis on Lyndale Avenue near Lake Street. But as they were flat broke, the couple soon packed up once again to make the long drive to Reno, where most of the

Karpis-Barker Gang had gone to live it up after Hamm's kidnapping. Edna thoroughly enjoyed joining the party.

On November 29, Verne Miller's body was discovered in a ditch outside Detroit, Michigan. He had been tortured to death in what appeared to be a gangland slaying. The reason for it is not known, but the botched escape attempt in Kansas City could have been part of it. Miller's grisly execution put a damper on the party spirits in Reno. The entire gang decided to drive back to Minnesota. A caravan of cars full of gangsters set out on December 1, heading toward the friendly confines of St. Paul. While driving through the mountains in Wyoming, Volney, most likely aided by a good amount of alcohol, took a curve a bit too fast, plunging them over a twenty-foot embankment. When the car came to rest, Volney scrambled out, horrified to see their guns and ammo scattered about after flying out the trunk. He was too busy gathering his arsenal to check on Edna, who was pretty banged up. She was scratched and bruised everywhere. She couldn't even see because of all the blood pouring from the bump to her head. They managed to get the car out of the ditch and drive it to Cheyenne, Wyoming, where the rest of the gang was waiting, anxiously wondering where they were. Fred Barker took one look at Edna and insisted that she should see a doctor. She adamantly refused. No way she wanted some nosy doctor finding out her real name, resulting in a ticket back to the penitentiary. So, Freddie did his best to patch her up, dressing her wounds. Edna was fuming mad the whole time, as Volney seemed more worried about the damage to his car than about her.

Back in St. Paul, with its gangster-friendly O'Connor System, it was easy to find a doctor who could be trusted to keep quiet. The doctor was horrified that Edna had not sought medical attention sooner. She had two cracked ribs and a fractured skull. The swelling in her head was so bad that the doctor could not give her the stitches she should have received. By delaying treatment, she'd run a big risk of getting an infection in such a gaping wound. But whatever Freddie did to clean it up must have been enough to avoid that. She had probably been in terrific pain as Volney drove over bumpy roads on the ride back to St. Paul. It says a lot about her life on the run that her desire to avoid capture greatly outweighed her need to get immediate medical treatment.

Edna and Volney moved into the first apartment they could find in St. Paul, but it was not up to her standards. They quickly moved into the Edgecumbe Court Apartments on Lexington Avenue, not far from the opulent mansions on exclusive Summit Avenue. The elegant Edgecumbe Court was extremely popular with crooks but was by far not the only place in the Twin Cities to hold clusters of gangsters. The Karpis-Barker Gang had rooms in several buildings, including the Grand Apartments at 1290 Grand Avenue and the Cle-Mar at 2092 Marshall Avenue. The Lowry Hotel, downtown at 339 North Wabasha Street, was a favorite with Alvin Karpis. The Commodore Hotel at 79 Western Avenue was not only home to noted St. Paul author F. Scott Fitzgerald but also hosted the Barkers and infamous Chicago mob boss Al Capone.

Perhaps the proprietors of all these establishments were unaware that they were catering to gangsters, but it seems more likely that they knew exactly who their clientele was. Most of the gangster men had recognizable faces due to wanted posters and photos published with sensational newspaper stories. Although the women almost always dealt with the rental process, the landlords had to have caught glimpses of these guys coming and going at all hours of the night, always sneaking out the back doors so as not to be seen by nosy neighbors. The majority of these landlords were most likely law-abiding citizens who would not normally look the other way from bank robbers, murderers and kidnappers. But this was the height of the Depression.

Edgecumbe Court Apartments in 2019. Known as the "Lamster's Hideout" because of the many criminals who rented apartments there, it was the home of Edna Murray and Volney Davis in December 1933. *Photo by Craig Frethem.*

The Commodore Hotel in 2019. Ma and Freddie Barker lived here in May 1933. *Photo by Craig Frethem.*

The bar in the Commodore Hotel in 2019. It looks much as it did back in the 1930s. *Photo by Craig Frethem.*

Reliable renters were a commodity that was hard to find. Gangsters seemed to be one of the few groups of people flush with enough money to afford the rent. And they regularly paid on time with nice big wads of cash. In an era before Social Security numbers, it was easy to give any fake name you liked on the lease. The Twin Cities landlords were certainly smart enough not to insist on any kind of background check. They were just happy to have cash to feed their families when times were hard and not really caring to think about how their renters had earned it.

Edna settled back into the Twin Cities nightlife despite her ill health. On Christmas Day 1933, Edna, Volney, Doc Barker, Harry Campbell and Wynona Burdette gathered at the Hollyhocks speakeasy in St. Paul to celebrate the fact that none of them would be in prison for the holidays. Edna and Volney spent New Year's Eve attending a movie in Minneapolis. The parties around the Twin Cities seemed to be nonstop. Most frequently, her party pals were Campbell; Burdette; Will Weaver with his moll, Myrtle Eaton; and Doc Barker. Edna even hung out with Fred Barker and his girlfriend, her nemesis, Paula Harmon. She also went to the Green Lantern, mixing with the powerful fixer Harry Sawyer and his wife, Gladys. It's unclear if Edna was aware yet about Harry's deceit when she had asked for his help in finding Doris.

The good times in Minnesota came to a sudden halt on January 17, 1934. Volney disappeared for a few hours that morning without telling Edna where he was going. But she suspected where he might have gone when she heard the news that banker Edward Bremer had been kidnapped at the corner of Lexington and Goodrich, not even two blocks from their apartment. Edna had known about the plans to kidnap Bremer, but perhaps the exact date was a surprise. Four days earlier, Alvin Karpis had shot Roy McCord, a Northwest Airlines radio operator whom he had mistaken for a policeman. Afterward, the gang held a meeting about the incident in her Edgecumbe Court apartment. Edna would later testify that she heard Freddie and Harry Sawyer agree that the kidnapping should be delayed until heat from the McCord shooting had died down. Karpis had a strict rule: "You didn't tell broads about jobs. Not ever." But Edna Murray seems to have been an exception to his rule, as Karpis trusted her to hang around during that meeting.

The day after the kidnapping, Volney returned home, demanding to know if anyone had been to their apartment while he had been gone.

Volney and Edna then took off for Will Weaver and Myrtle Eaton's place at the Kennington Apartments. As soon as they arrived, she was ordered to immediately take Wynona Burdette and Paula Harmon back to her place at Edgecumbe Court. It was her job to keep the two women hidden away from the police. Karpis worried that they'd spill the beans if captured. Edna must have been pretty unhappy about having Paula in her apartment, but she obeyed her orders, taking the women home. It didn't last long. Volney quickly showed up to tell the women that the heat was on. Harry Sawyer had tipped off the gang about a warning he'd received from his sources within the St. Paul Police Department: well-known gangster homes were going to be searched hoping to catch the Bremer kidnapping culprits. With Edgecumbe Court being so close to the crime scene, it was a good bet that Edna's place would be high on the list of spots to be raided. Volney escorted the women to Harry Sawyer's farm out in the country on Snail Lake in Shoreview. Sawyer was pretty much an honorary member of the Karpis-Barker Gang, so many of them had hung out there frequently to party or to hide from pesky law enforcement. In fact, FBI files claim that Sawyer purchased the farm in 1933 with loot the gang stole from the bank in Fairbury, Nebraska. It was his reward for helping to launder the stolen cash. Decades later, subsequent owners remodeling Sawyer's old farm home found two secret tunnels and many odd items stashed in the walls, such as liquor bottles and vintage 1930s prescription eyeglasses.

But it was determined that even Sawyer's secluded rural farm was not far enough away. The women were told that they needed to beat it for Chicago. Edna, still quite ill, did not feel up to driving. Volney enlisted George Ziegler to chauffeur her there. Not far into Wisconsin, they came across Paula Harmon and Wynona Burette parked at the side of the road, crying hysterically, too frightened to drive themselves. With some coaxing from Ziegler, the two women finally got in the back seat of his car so they could continue. Once in Chicago, Ziegler found Edna an apartment. Wynona and Paula, unable to find a place on their own, moved in shortly thereafter. Predictably, it didn't go well. Paula repeatedly antagonized Edna with more stories about Volney running around with other women. Paula ignored Edna's orders to stop, ramping up the needling by once again accusing her and Volney of being leeches, living off Fred Barker's money. Edna finally had enough, landing a good solid punch on Paula's face while screaming, "Get your ass out of my apartment! There's no way I'm going to live with you!" Paula immediately moved out. Wynona left with her, most likely not wanting to risk getting on the bad side of Edna too. Fred and Volney showed up a few times over the next three weeks wearing bulletproof vests and acting nervously. When Fred asked her about Paula's battered face, Edna just smiled and responded that he would have to go ask Paula. Obviously, she had no regrets about beating up Fred's moll.

Soon after Ed Bremer was released, Volney, Doc, Freddy, Karpis and Ziegler showed up at Edna's Chicago apartment, all acting like nervous cats. She had always known the gang to be cool and confident after a job. Their anxiety and nerves told her that they realized they may have finally overstepped with the Bremer kidnapping back in St. Paul.

The gang split up, with Edna and Volney heading to Aurora, Illinois, where she once again sought medical attention, this time for severely infected ingrown toenails and for what she called female problems, probably some sort of venereal disease given to her by the ever-unfaithful Volney Davis. In the middle of March, Ma Barker showed up at their door, begging Volney to come back to Chicago to help Freddie and Alvin, who were in great pain due to surgery to remove their fingerprints. Volney was irritated, but as he thought of her like a mother, he dutifully obeyed. Edna was perturbed with him for leaving. She wanted him there taking care of her! Volney did attend when she had surgery to free up her ingrown toenails; however, the tough guy fainted halfway through the procedure.

On April 25, Volney returned from Chicago only to order Edna to move out for a few days. The Dillinger Gang had been in a pretty serious shootout at Little Bohemia Lodge in northern Wisconsin a few days earlier. In a subsequent car chase, Dillinger Gang member John "Red" Hamilton had been shot. The Karpis-Barker Gang was doing the Dillinger Gang a solid favor, giving the members a safe place to hide out during the manhunt that followed. Edna came home a few days later to find shocking conditions. After many hours of futile attempts to treat his wounds, Hamilton had died in her apartment. Upon entering, a strong odor turned her stomach. Disinfectant powder was everywhere, even on her bed, which was most likely where Hamilton had passed. Dirty dishes, bloody linens and bandages were strewn everywhere. When she opened her closet door, a muddy shovel, the one the gang used to bury Hamilton, fell out and hit her foot. Edna was extremely distraught at the knowledge that Hamilton had been placed in an unmarked grave. When gangsters died on the lam, they were often buried with no fanfare. Their family were seldom told about the death, much less where their loved one was buried. The less information out there, the less the chance of being captured. This was one aspect of the gangster lifestyle that did not sit well with Edna Murray. She had a morbid fear that she too might one day end up in a potter's field, unmourned in an unmarked grave.

But worst of all, John Dillinger, his best friend Homer Van Meter, Doc Barker and Harry Campbell were all still there. The four gangsters, along with Volney Davis, listened to the radio all day, following the intensive nationwide search for Dillinger. As with Verne Miller after the Kansas City Massacre, Edna found herself once again with the country's hottest criminal hiding out in her apartment. She set about cleaning up the mess, all the while avoiding Dillinger and Van Meter as much as she could. Neither ever put down their Tommy guns, and both were wearing bulletproof vests. They seemed to her like caged animals. Edna did not like Dillinger because he gave her "the creeps with his sneering, snarling, crooked smile and his piercing eyes."

When Dillinger and Van Meter finally left, Edna went to pick up her now eighteen-year-old son, Preston. Volney and Doc Barker went to see Doc Moran to have plastic surgery on their faces and get their fingerprints removed, even though they had seen how poorly it had gone for Fred and Alvin. When Edna met up with them, Volney tried to convince her to have the same operations, but seeing their intense pain and how badly the surgeries had been botched, Edna refused. Besides, she thought she was a real beauty as is, and there was no way she would mess with that!

Most of the gang went to Ohio to rest up in remote cabins on Lake Erie. But there wasn't much relaxing going on, as the gang was completely on edge, bickering among themselves. One day, Edna overheard a very loud argument between Volney and Fred. She had no idea what the fuss had been about, but it was enough that Volney swore to her that they were done with the Karpis-Barker Gang. Edna was worried sick. She knew that Freddie would not hesitate to kill Volney over the falling out despite being friends since childhood. And since Edna knew so much about the two kidnappings, she could logically be next. While the couple hurriedly began to pack up, Harry Sawyer, who was visiting the gang from Minnesota, showed up at their door. The St. Paul fixer gave them some advice and helped them with making their escape from the angry Fred Barker and Alvin Karpis.

They decided that the empty stretches of Montana were a good place to go to hide out. They stopped in Minnesota on the way for a brief respite in the friendly confines of St. Paul but didn't stay very long, as they risked running into their new enemies and former friends, the Karpis-Barker Gang. Driving through North Dakota, Volney once again drove too fast for slippery roads and flipped the car. Edna landed in the hospital. As with her previous car accident, she was more worried about the doctors finding out her real name than she was about her injuries. Volney, tired of life on the run, opened a tavern/dance hall in Glasgow, Montana. But they couldn't seem to actually settle down. They left frequently to knock around the Midwest, visiting family in Kansas City several times, where Volney's reckless driving, again aided by a good share of alcohol, caused Edna to be injured in yet a third car accident.

They arrived in Kansas City, Missouri, on February 2, 1935, to visit Edna's sister Doris and Jess Doyle and to handle some important business. For Volney, that meant dropping off his stolen Pontiac at the garage to be serviced. For Edna, it was a trip to the beauty parlor. That same day, they read in the paper the unsettling news that they had both been indicted back in St. Paul for the Bremer kidnapping.

February 6, 1935, was the day that things finally came crashing down for Edna Murray. The evening before, they'd had a nice dinner, gone for a walk and then went to bed for what would end up being their last night together. They were awoken early that morning by Jess Doyle pounding on their door with very distressing news: Doris had been arrested for shooting and killing a woman. Edna was stunned to hear that her sister was accused of murder.

Volney left later that morning to pick up his Pontiac. Edna was in an anxious mood all day. Why had her sister shot that woman? Would Doris spill the beans about them while in custody? And what about the Bremer kidnapping indictment back in St. Paul? She became even more worried when Volney failed to return from picking up his car. At 6:00 p.m., she took a cab to a spot near the United Motors Service garage but was unable to peek inside to see if she could spot the Pontiac. Still sensing that something was terribly wrong, she tore back home to pack up and run, as she had done so many times before. Life on the lam had taught her how to move quickly, only taking what she really needed. Edna and Jess then spent several hours driving around Kansas City trying to spot Volney. Unable to find any trace of her longtime love, she was now completely convinced that he had been nabbed by the cops. Edna and Jess decide to drive to Pittsburg, Kansas, to the home of her brother Harry Stanley. Harry must have been quite stunned at the turn of events when they arrived at his door at 1:00 a.m. He certainly knew that his two sisters were no angels. In fact, he and his wife, Sybil, had sheltered many of Edna's gangland pals in the past, including Alvin Karpis and the Barker brothers. But now he learned that both sisters were potentially looking at life sentences: one for murder and the other for kidnapping.

Early the next morning, Jess decided to run when he saw his name in the morning paper, listed as a wanted fugitive. Edna, already in bad health and feeling even sicker from all the stress, declined to go with him. Harry went out to buy some alcohol to calm everyone's nerves but ran back ten minutes later to report that someone was chasing Jess and shooting at his car. Just then, a car full of very serious-looking men drove up to the Stanley home. Two special agents with the FBI walked in to arrest everyone. Edna stood up, tossed her .32-caliber automatic pistol on the sofa and gave up.

She was in no mood to cooperate while in jail. When a female guard ordered her to strip naked while a male guard peeked from around the corner, the feisty Edna got nasty, shoving her soiled sanitary napkin in the matron's chest. Her health was going downhill, she was facing life in prison and her lover, Volney Davis, had been arrested too. Sitting in her cell, nervously chain-smoking, Edna was miserable. She was somewhat cheered by hearing the good news that the murder charges against Doris had been dropped.

EDNA MURRAY AND JESS Doyle were flown to St. Paul to be tried for the kidnapping of Edward Bremer. Volney Davis had managed to escape custody after his arrest and was on the run. Mastermind Alvin Karpis had avoided capture so far too. Freddy and Ma were dead. The kidnapping trial for Edna, Jess, Doc Barker, Byron Bolton and four others started on April 15, 1935, in the federal courthouse on Fifth Street, right next door to Edward Bremer's office in the Commercial State Bank. Fifteen days later on May 6, the kidnapping charges against Edna and Jess were completely dropped with no explanation. The pair celebrated by holding court for reporters in the matron's lounge of the Ramsey County jail on Kellogg Boulevard and Wabasha Street. They laughed, told stories and posed for photographs for the gathered group of journalists. And Edna was quite photogenic with her perfect makeup, bleached blond hair and stylish gingham dress. Smoking many cigarettes, they freely spoke about the kidnapping. When asked how she felt, Edna proclaimed, "Well, I feel swell, of course." She added that she had been confident of her exoneration from the start. However, she had not foreseen the charges being completely dismissed.

While Edna was released from the kidnapping charges, she was not free to go blithely on her way. There was still the matter of the imprisonment for armed robbery that she had yet to finish. Edna was quite vocal in her displeasure at the prospect of being sent back to prison. She insisted to anyone who would listen that she was innocent. When the subject came up during her press conference in the Ramsey County jail, she told reporters, "I'm not guilty. I was framed…I am perfectly innocent of the charge."

In their notes, FBI agents expressed that they suspected Edna was being less than truthful during her interrogations. She steadfastly refused to say anything that would incriminate her dearest "Curly" and several others in the Karpis-Barker Gang—that is, until Byron Bolton, Jess Doyle and Volney Davis began talking. Volney had been recaptured in June and sent to St. Paul too. Bitterly figuring that she had nothing to lose anymore, Edna then spilled what she knew. She even testified in the January 1936 kidnapping trials of Will Weaver and Harry Sawyer.

Her cooperation didn't seem to do much good. The Minnesota court ordered her sent back to Missouri to complete her twenty-five-year sentence with two extra years added on for those three escapes. A sheriff was assigned to drive her back. Not long after crossing out of Minnesota into Iowa, Edna's string of bad luck with cars continued when the sheriff collided with another car. Luckily, this time it was just bumps and bruises. And for once, alcohol was not a factor.

FOR WELL OVER A decade, Edna had lived a hectic, dangerous life of constantly being on the run. Worn down, tired and ill, she made the choice to just do her time—no more trying to escape. Back at the Missouri Penitentiary, Edna "Rabbit" Murray, the Kissing Bandit, the Triple Escape Queen, the glamorous Flapper Bandit, simply became prisoner no. 28973. She was assigned to share a cell with Blanche Barrow, the sister-in-law of Clyde Barrow. The two women became fast friends, trading stories of their respective lives of crime: Edna with the Karpis-Barker Gang and Blanche while running with Bonnie and Clyde. Edna would laughingly refer to Blanche as her "pen pal."

Her good behavior paid off. She was paroled after five years on December 20, 1940. She moved to San Francisco to be near other members of the Stanley family, who had settled in various parts of California. There she married her fifth husband, Carl Memmott. In 1946, she became a grandmother with the birth of Preston's daughter, Pamela Lou Paden. The Memmott marriage didn't last long either, probably because Edna had always had a hard time staying faithful to anyone but Volney Davis. She then married her sixth and final husband, Henry "Hank" Potter, a service station attendant. Living in San Francisco, she must have been reminded of her past many times when she looked out into the bay to see the prison on Alcatraz Island, where her old flame Volney "Curly" Davis and his pal Alvin "Creepy" Karpis were serving life sentences.

Edna's criminal past came knocking on her door on July 8, 1954. She was served with a subpoena to appear in court in St. Paul to testify. Volney Davis was appealing his conviction for the Bremer kidnapping. Even though she was living in San Francisco, she had made no effort all those years to go visit Volney at Alcatraz. Yet now she was excited at the prospect of seeing him again in St. Paul. Or maybe it was just St. Paul that she was thrilled to see. Either way, Martha Edna Potter, the San Francisco service station attendant's housewife, flew to Minnesota to appear one last time as Edna Murray, the Kissing Bandit, member of the infamous Karpis-Barker Gang. Volney's hearing took place in the same federal courthouse in downtown St. Paul where Edna, Volney, Doc Barker, "Creepy" Karpis and several others had stood trial in 1935. Back then, she had been thin, sickly and scared at the prospect of life in prison. On this beautiful July day in 1954, Edna was a radiant vision as she took the stand in the fancy new outfit she had purchased especially for the occasion, her hair and makeup perfect. Sitting just a few feet from her former beau, she retold her part in the Bremer kidnapping and what she knew about Volney's actions during that time. She was stunned to see how life in Alcatraz had changed her handsome "Curly." He was pale and thin, his gorgeous, chestnut-brown curls had turned gray and sparse.

Edna flew straight from St. Paul to Oklahoma to visit her son, Preston; his wife, Naomi; and her granddaughter, Pam. According to Pam, Edna arrived from St. Paul "wound for sound!" Edna gushed on and on about old associates like Harry Sawyer and "fat-witted" Paula Harmon (yes, Edna still held a grudge there after all those years). She annoyed Naomi by endlessly relating tales of her time with the Karpis-Barker Gang to young, impressionable Pammie Lou. But Edna's visit to Minnesota had been an exciting trip into her past, and she couldn't stop talking about it.

While Edna chose to give up her gangster lifestyle, she looked back on her career with lots of affection. According to Pam, the only thing her grandmother seemed to regret was the time spent in prison. In fact, Edna often insisted that she was a "good girl" who had just gotten some bad breaks. Pam has fond memories of watching her grandmother Edna telling tales of her shady past to anyone who would listen, laughing heartily at her own stories, slapping her knee and throwing back her head to reveal her mouth full of gold teeth. Edna seemed to look back at her gangster days through a rosy glow, conveniently forgetting the hardship, fear and death.

Edna gave up crime, but she never completely turned away from several bad habits she picked up in her wild youth. Pam recalled that Grandma Edna always somehow managed to have a boyfriend within five minutes of arriving in Oklahoma, even when she had a husband back in San Francisco. She never could be without masculine attention for very long. Pam also noted that she "always seemed to have a beer in one hand and a cigarette in the other." When her son, Preston, was dying of an inherited form of emphysema, Edna came to visit. After she left, Naomi noticed that much of her dying husband's pain medication was missing. Her mother-in-law, the Kissing Bandit, was suspect number one.

It's hard to say why Edna chose this criminal life. She was an escapee almost the entire time but seemed to relish every moment of it. During the Depression, she had fancy clothes, all the liquor she wanted and the glory of hanging out with infamous gangsters. In an interview for the documentary film *Gangsterland*, Pam said her infamous grandmother "was a 'Drama Queen' long before it became popular." She guessed that Edna may have been bipolar, and most certainly she had a drug and drinking problem; perhaps she would have had a much different life if she could have gotten proper medical and mental health treatment.

By the mid-1960s, Edna's hard living finally caught up with her. She spent about a week in the hospital, enduring several operations for intestinal ulcerations, blood clots and gangrene in both legs. She also suffered from hypertension, osteoporosis and emphysema. Edna "Rabbit" Murray, the infamous Kissing Bandit, passed away on April 13, 1966, at age sixty-seven. She is buried at the Golden Gate Cemetery in San Francisco under the name Martha Edna Potter.

Ultimately, for better or worse, Edna looked back with few regrets, choosing to remember the glamor and the fun, conveniently overlooking her wrongdoing. For whatever reason, she had no fear, thriving on the danger and excitement of her life with Volney Davis and the Karpis-Barker Gang.

VOLNEY DAVIS

Volney Everett Davis was born on January 29, 1902, in the Cherokee Nation area of the Indian territory—a place that would later become Tahlequah, Oklahoma. (Oklahoma did not become a state until 1907.) Davis must have been a bit spoiled in childhood, as he had five sisters and was the only boy out of six children. While Volney was still fairly young, the Davis family moved to Tulsa, Oklahoma. Davis soon made many friends at his local elementary school—just not the right kind of friends. He fell in the with the Central Park Gang, whose members included future Karpis-Barker gangsters Harry Campbell and the Barker brothers, Arthur and Freddie. Young Volney was especially close to Arthur "Doc" Barker. He spent so much time over at the Barker home that he began calling Kate Barker "Mother" just as if he were one of her boys. He continued to call her "Mother" for the rest of her life.

At seventeen years old, Volney was a good-looking man with thick, curly, chestnut-colored hair. He readily flashed a large grin that would light up his handsome face, showing off a mouthful of beautiful white teeth. Volney had already gotten into plenty of trouble committing petty crimes as part of the Central Park Gang, but it was at this age that he finally landed in jail. In February 1919, he was sentenced to three years for grand larceny, having pleaded guilty to robbing fifty dollars from a shoe store and auto casings from a gas station. Davis soon demonstrated that he had a knack for jailbreaks, managing to escape and be recaptured a few times before he was

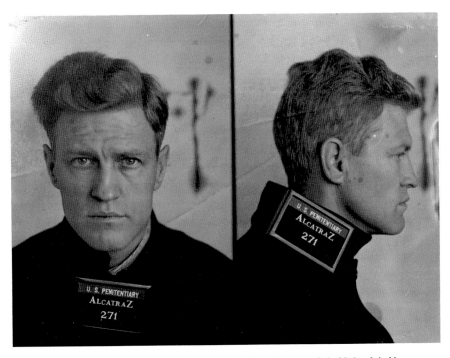

Volney Davis, shortly after he entered Alcatraz in 1935. *Courtesy of the National Archives at San Francisco.*

finally shipped off to the Oklahoma State Penitentiary, where busting out wouldn't be so easy.

Paroled in June 1921, Volney Davis didn't keep clean very long. Just two months later, on August 26, he and Doc Barker committed their first major robbery, burglarizing a construction site at St. John's Hospital in Tulsa. It was also their first murder. Things went smoothly at first. Volney had been employed there as a construction worker, so he knew the layout very well. However, the night watchman, Sheriff Thomas J. Sherrill, surprised them while the burglary was in progress. In the flurry of bullets that followed, Sherill was shot and killed, leaving behind a wife and nine children. A little over four months later, on January 8, 1922, Volney, Doc and several members of the Central Park Gang were cornered by police. In the ensuing gun battle, two more people died: a fellow gang member and a police officer. Doc Barker and two others were arrested. Volney managed to avoid capture that day but was quickly arrested a short time later. He sat in jail for nearly a year awaiting trial. On February 3, 1923, he was convicted for his part in the robbery and murder of Sheriff Sherrill. At just twenty-one years old, he received a sentence of life in prison.

Volney Davis didn't like prison. He did get visits and Christmas gifts from his sweetheart, Edna Murray, a waitress he had met three years earlier at an Oklahoma café. But the idea of spending the rest of his life behind bars just didn't sit well with him. On January 8, 1925, Davis and several other prisoners jumped the fence and made their escape. He reunited with Edna in Kansas City. While he had a talent for busting out of prison, he wasn't very good yet at staying out. Their togetherness lasted only a few weeks. The police raided Edna's apartment one day looking for illegal alcohol. When fingerprints were taken, Volney was discovered to be an escaped con and sent back to the penitentiary in Oklahoma.

DAVIS SAT IN PRISON for the next seven years until November 3, 1932, when he was released on a twenty-month leave of absence. This kind of temporary release was fairly common in Oklahoma at the time. Edna Murray's granddaughter, Pam Paden Tippet, claimed that Doc Barker had arranged for the leave. Alvin Karpis inferred pretty much the same thing in his autobiography, hinting that the decision to grant the leave had been heavily influenced by a $1,500 bribe given to prison officials. Of course, Volney Davis had no intention of returning to his cell when his leave from prison was up.

Doc Barker also helped to arrange Volney's reunion with his sweetheart, Edna Murray, freshly escaped from prison herself. Through a series of letters, Doc was able to engineer the lovebirds' reunion in Missouri, where Edna was hiding out. The couple then went to Chicago, where they met up with his old childhood chums, Freddie and Doc, who introduced them to their new friend Alvin "Creepy" Karpis and other members of the newly formed Karpis-Barker Gang: Frank "Jelly" Nash, Earl Christman, Eddie Green and sheriff turned gangster Verne Miller. Volney Davis and his Central Park Gang friends from Oklahoma now made up a good portion of one of the most notorious bands of Depression-era criminals.

About one month later, the Karpis-Barker Gang robbed the Third Northwestern National Bank in Minneapolis. Karpis hadn't gotten to know Davis very well yet, plus he felt that Doc's old childhood chum had joined the gang too late to be included in such a big job. Instead, Volney was assigned the task of taking care of Ma Barker, who was in Chicago and had come down with heart palpitations. Karpis claimed in his autobiography that he had been the one to see to Ma, but Robert Livesey, who spent years interviewing Karpis for his other book, *On the Rock*, believes that it was actually Volney who took care of Ma. It made sense for him to be the one to see to her needs since she considered him to be like another son and he was in Chicago anyway. When she felt better, he took her to Reno, Nevada, where the whole gang met to celebrate Christmas.

Volney Davis was, however, invited to participate in the next Karpis-Barker bank job when they hit the First National Bank in Fairbury, Nebraska. But when the gang kidnapped wealthy beer magnate William Hamm Jr. in St. Paul on June 15, 1933, Davis was visiting family back in Missouri. The kidnapping created such a national stir that he was quite happy to have the alibi of being several states away when it happened. Byron Bolton later provided the FBI with a list detailing how Hamm's ransom money had been split up. Davis, who denied having anything to do with the kidnapping, was listed as receiving $700. Maybe it was just a friendly loan, but maybe Davis wasn't as innocent as he claimed. While it is true that he wasn't there when the snatch happened, it's also true that he had visited St. Paul on at least one occasion during the time it was being planned. He had stayed in the apartment building at 204 Vernon Street that was occupied by Doc Barker, Fred Barker, Alvin Karpis, Charlie Fitzgerald, William Weaver and George Ziegler—all players in Hamm's kidnapping. Davis may have helped with planning the kidnapping or, at the very least, knew about it in advance and did nothing to stop it.

Volney came back home to the Chicago apartment he shared with Edna, only to have Verne Miller show up after the botched Kansas City Massacre. Miller and Pretty Boy Floyd had gone to Kansas City to help free Frank "Jelly" Nash from custody. Things went horribly wrong, resulting in Nash, three police officers and a federal agent getting killed. Edna and Volney were both quite unhappy with having Miller in their apartment—too much heat. Miller was now the most sought-after gangster in the country. Volney reluctantly agreed to help him hide for several days until things died down, perhaps because he was still trying to prove himself to be a loyal member of the Karpis-Barker Gang. But the heat didn't die down. The country was horrified by the bloody events in Kansas City. At the time, agents with the Bureau of Investigation did not have the authority to carry firearms or make arrests. Bureau chief J. Edgar Hoover had been working for some time to get that changed. Hoover vigorously used the Kansas City Massacre to further his cause, maintaining that there would not have been so much loss of life if his agents had carried guns. One year later, in June 1934, Congress finally agreed, giving federal agents statutory authority to carry guns and make arrests.

After a fruitless visit to St. Paul, Minnesota, to try to locate Edna's sister Doris, Volney and Edna headed back to Chicago. Volney did love Edna, but he had a hard time being faithful to her, a fact that Fred Barker's girlfriend Paula Harmon loved lording over Edna. Finally having had enough of Volney's selfishness and philandering, Edna took the car and headed west to Minneapolis, where she finally found Doris and her boyfriend, Jess Doyle. Inevitably, Volney came running to Minnesota a few weeks later, showing up at Doris's south Minneapolis apartment, begging for Edna's forgiveness. The romance of it all convinced her to take him back.

Edna and Volney stayed in Minnesota a short time, but as they were flat broke, they soon drove to Reno to tap Alvin Karpis and Fred Barker for some cash. The gang had gone there once again to party, this time to celebrate Hamm's kidnapping. A few weeks later, the Karpis-Barker Gang decided to drive back to Minnesota on December 1, 1933. Normally Edna loved Volney Davis's dangerous, cavalier ways, but his careless driving caused her to be seriously injured in a car accident when he took a curve a bit too fast. It didn't help that Volney was probably drunk at the time.

ON JANUARY 17, 1934, Volney Davis participated in the biggest job of his career when the Karpis-Barker Gang kidnapped St. Paul banker Edward

Bremer. The kidnapping went down at the intersection of Lexington and Goodrich, just one and a half blocks from the Edgecumbe Court Apartments, where Volney and Edna were living at the time. After Bremer dropped his daughter off at school, his car was boxed in by two other cars. Volney and Doc jumped out of the backseat of the car behind Bremer, opened the banker's front car doors and forced him to the floorboards. Of course, Bremer's car stalled when he was knocked over. The engine died in those vintage 1930s cars if your foot wasn't on either the clutch or gas pedal at all times. Doc was busy pistol-whipping their struggling victim while Davis tried to restart the engine. Unfortunately, he could not find the electric starter button on Bremer's luxury car. The two gangsters began to panic, causing Doc to hit the still struggling banker on the head even harder. They were worried that if they didn't get the car out of there soon, someone in the densely populated area would notice the action and call the authorities. Ed Bremer was now bleeding profusely from his head wounds. Realizing that the hyped-up gangsters would keep beating him until they got the car restarted, Bremer reached up with the bloody hand that he had been using to try to shield his head and pushed the electric starter button for Davis. Bremer's bloody fingerprint was recovered from the button when the cops found his car after the gang ditched it.

Volney Davis spent the next three weeks running errands for the Karpis-Barker Gang while the crew waited for the ransom money, going back and forth between Minnesota and Bensenville, the Chicago suburb where Bremer was being held. One of his jobs was to make sure the gang members' girlfriends were out of reach from the law, mostly because Karpis worried that the women would crack and talk if caught. Most of the women were eventually sent to Chicago, including Volney's sweetheart, Edna Murray. The ransom was finally paid and Bremer released on February 7, 1934. The gang was flush with money, but it was marked money.

In late April, Volney Davis helped out in a rare instance of cooperation between the Karpis-Barker Gang and the Dillinger Gang. On April 22, 1934, Dillinger's gang had a bloody shootout with the FBI at the Little Bohemia Lodge in northern Wisconsin. An innocent bystander, a police officer and a federal agent were killed. Dillinger; his right-hand man, Homer Van Meter; and John "Red" Hamilton headed back to Minnesota. But while they were crossing the spiral bridge in Hastings, deputies recognized Dillinger and opened fire. The three gangsters got away, but not before Hamilton was gravely wounded with a bullet through his back. They headed to Chicago, where Davis allowed Dillinger, Van Meter and Hamilton to hide out in his apartment. Hamilton was treated for his bullet wound but could not be saved, dying in Volney and Edna's bed. The next morning, Volney, Doc, Dillinger, Van Meter and Harry Campbell hauled Hamilton's body to an isolated area near Oswego, Illinois. Before covering the body with dirt, they poured ten cans of lye on Hamilton's face and hands to conceal his identity.

The nationwide manhunt for the Dillinger Gang was massive. J. Edgar Hoover was desperate to find his current Public Enemy Number One. Hoover had been humiliated by the events at Little Bohemia and was still burning up over the Kansas City Massacre. Now that Hamilton was dead, Volney Davis wanted Dillinger and Van Meter gone. He had no desire to be arrested because of their troubles. But the pair couldn't leave without a car, so Volney and Edna drove Doc Barker's car over to some guys they knew in the auto theft business. They bought a nice big Ford that Volney drove back while Edna drove Doc's Buick.

Things got worse that night when Volney and Doc found out the distressing news that their money launderer, John "Boss" Mclaughlin, had been arrested for passing some of the Bremer ransom money. They worried that their launderer would spill the beans about how it had been the Karpis-Barker Gang that had perpetrated the kidnapping in St. Paul. The last thing Volney and Edna needed was getting their apartment raided. Not only were they sheltering Dillinger and Van Meter, but there was also another large chunk of incriminating Bremer ransom sitting in their closet.

Everyone holed up in the apartment was on edge, sitting in the dark, expecting G-men to swoop down on them at any moment. Volney would occasionally take a short walk outside to scout for potential trouble. He came tearing back into the apartment from one such excursion shouting at Edna to pack her bags and run. Two men had gotten out of a car on one end of the block, and three more came out of another car at the other end. Doc Barker screamed at Volney to calm down while at the same time ordering Edna to stay put. But Doc was panicking too. He shoved his Tommy gun out the window to cut down the approaching men, no questions asked. Dillinger and Van Meter had cooler heads. Dillinger hissed at Doc to settle down and not do anything until they knew it was feds for sure. Dillinger, Van Meter, Doc, Volney, Edna and Harry Campbell all sat, sweating in the dark with anticipation of the gun battle to come. A third car then pulled up right out front. Two men from that car knocked on the door. It was Karpis-Barker Gang member Jimmie Wilson and a friend who informed them that there was nothing to fear—the mysterious men, obviously not G-men, were gone. Early the next morning, John Dillinger and Homer Van Meter took off in the stolen Ford. Both gangs were relieved to see the last of each other.

Afterward, Volney and Doc Barker traveled to see the infamous Doc Moran to get their fingerprints burned off and have some plastic surgery to look less like their wanted posters. The surgery on their hands had been excruciating. Their fingertips looked like raw meat. And all that agony was for nothing—when his fingers finally healed up, Volney's fingerprints came back as plainly as they had been before. When Edna caught up with them, she didn't think their faces looked any different.

After knocking around the country for a while, sometimes separately, sometimes together, Volney and Edna ended up in a remote area of Ohio where most of the gang had gone to relax in rental cabins on Lake Erie. But tensions were running high, resulting in the gang members quarreling among themselves. One day, several of them went to a nearby club to play horseshoes. Edna left the festivities to go inside when she heard a loud argument erupt outside. Volney Davis and Freddie Barker were having a heated exchange, apparently over something that Ma Barker had said about Volney. According to Edna, Volney ended the fight by shouting at Freddie, "I wouldn't bring my mother into an argument. You would be a motherfucker if you didn't hold up for your own mother, but I still say she's a damn liar." Angry, Freddie and Alvin Karpis left. Volney swore to Edna that they were done with the Barker brothers and that "old lady." The next day, he went to Freddie to demand his share of the Bremer ransom. Whatever the argument had been about, it was the end of Volney Davis's association with his childhood buddies and the Karpis-Barker Gang.

VOLNEY AND EDNA EVENTUALLY settled in Glasgow, Montana, where Volney opened a gambling and dance hall. Edna's son, Preston, helped out with it. But with Volney growing more and more paranoid about getting caught, they would leave Montana often, entrusting the dance hall to his co-owner and young Preston. In early January 1935, they were in Kansas City when they heard about Doc Barker being arrested in Chicago. Volney was very sad to hear the news about his former best friend. But he was really torn up when he heard about the deaths of Freddie and Ma. Kate Barker had truly been like a mother to him. And despite his falling out with Freddie and Doc, he and the Barker brothers had been through a lot together.

On January 22, 1935, Volney Davis and Edna Murray were indicted in federal court back in St. Paul for the Bremer kidnapping. Paula Harmon,

Fred Barker's drunken girlfriend, had been arrested for disorderly conduct. In custody, she happily ratted out Volney one last time, telling the authorities that he had been involved in the Bremer kidnapping. After reading in the newspaper about the indictment and warrants for their arrest, Volney told Edna it was just a "tough break, Rabbit."

On January 30, 1935, Davis participated in the last of his many robberies when he and two other men hit a bank trust in Independence, Kansas. He was captured in Kansas City, Missouri, by federal agents on February 6, 1935. He and Edna had arrived in the city only four days earlier to take his latest stolen car in for servicing. FBI agents picked him up when he arrived outside the United Motors Service garage to claim his Pontiac. The agents mistakenly thought they had captured Jess Doyle, who had also been indicted in the Bremer kidnapping. Davis saw no reason to correct them. The next day, he and his FBI escorts boarded a plane headed to St. Paul, where "Jess Doyle" was to stand trial. Davis most certainly knew that when he arrived in Minnesota, the mistaken identity would be cleared up, but he continued to keep his mouth shut. Although he felt confident that the case against him in the Bremer kidnapping was weak, there was still plenty of evidence to send him away for several other crimes, including bank robbery and murder. So, when their flight was forced to land prematurely in Yorkville, Illinois, Davis used the subsequent confusion as an opportunity to once again escape custody. He knocked out a guard, stole a car and ran.

Davis was on the run, while Edna Murray was up in Minnesota, on trial for the Bremer kidnapping. He was free for nearly four months before being recaptured by the famous G-man Melvin Purvis in Chicago on June 1, 1935. The following day, he was flown to Minneapolis. On June 3, he was finally booked in St. Paul for the kidnapping of Edward Bremer. His confidence that he would not be convicted faded when he heard about Byron Bolton's testimony from the April kidnapping trials. Bolton had named Davis as participating. Edna was furious at Bolton for ratting on her lover. She was adamant that her "Curly" was innocent, saying that Volney could not have been at the kidnapping because "he didn't get up early enough" that day. She claimed that he was still in bed with her when it happened. Speaking with reporters, Edna explained why she thought Bolton would lie about Volney. "He is a sneak," she averred. "He is trying to escape the hot seat for the Valentine's Day Massacre down in Chicago." But later, Alvin Karpis would also state that Davis had been present during the Bremer kidnapping. And Edna changed her tune a bit years later. When visiting her son in Oklahoma, Edna often spoke of her life with the Karpis-Barker Gang. She gave her granddaughter Pam the distinct impression that when it came to the Bremer kidnapping, Volney "did his share all the way around."

Confronted with the evidence against him, Davis saw the handwriting on the wall and began cooperating with the FBI, telling them what he knew about the Karpis-Barker Gang. He seemed very remorseful while sitting in his Ramsey County jailhouse cell in downtown St. Paul. He was tired of running. In a letter to his parents during that time, he expressed how awful it had been to not stay in contact with his family, "the only ones in this world that really love me." (Don't know what Edna would have thought of that statement!) He went on to ask them to tell the young boys in the family to "take a lesson from my experience and never touch anything that don't belong to them. For a man can get more enjoyment out of ten dollars he has earned honestly than he can a thousand got dishonestly. I know from sad experience."

Davis was arraigned on June 7, 1935, at the federal courthouse in St. Paul. He appeared without counsel and pleaded guilty to the Bremer kidnapping. Four days later, he was sentenced to life imprisonment. He was never charged with any of the holdups he committed while part of the Karpis-Barker Gang.

After a short intake time in Leavenworth, Volney Davis entered Alcatraz on October 25, 1935, as prisoner no. AZ-271. His intake exam revealed him to be five feet, nine and a half inches, weighing 142 pounds and in excellent health—surprising results given his chain smoking, heavy drinking and stressful life of constant running. His intelligence was rated as above average despite having only a sixth-grade education. Doc Barker, who had arrived in Alcatraz before Volney, refused to have anything to do with his former best friend.

Davis was concerned when he heard the following summer that Alvin Karpis was on his way to Alcatraz. He perhaps had good reason to be worried. Davis had not only spilled information to the FBI, but he had also testified against other members of the gang as well. Always paranoid in the best of times, he feared this cooperation would make him a target in prison. Davis was certain that Karpis would kill him. Davis tried to befriend Karpis when he showed up, but "Creepy" would have none of it. Karpis highly suspected that Davis was the one who had ratted him out as the mastermind of Hamm's kidnapping. Plus Doc had immediately warned Karpis upon arrival that Davis "was poison" and not to be trusted. All of his efforts to win back Karpis's trust failed, culminating in a prison yard fistfight between the two. Davis, a former boxer, got the upper hand, but both men ended up in

Courtroom 317, where Alvin Karpis, Doc Barker, Edna Murray and Volney Davis were put on trial for the Bremer kidnapping. *Photo by Bick Smith.*

solitary. Although Davis provoked the fight, he thought it unfair that he was punished too, as he had allowed Karpis to throw the first punch.

Other than that one fight and the occasional bootlegging while running the prison print shop, Volney Davis was a model prisoner. But that doesn't mean he was happy with being in Alcatraz. In January 1952, he sent an appeal to the U.S. District Court in Minnesota regarding his 1935 conviction for the Bremer kidnapping. He asked for his sentence to be eliminated or reduced on the grounds that he had not completely understood his constitutional rights when he had pleaded guilty without representation by a lawyer. It took a few years for him to get his hearing, probably because it required some effort to gather up the remains of the Karpis-Barker Gang and others to come testify. In early July 1954, the now fifty-two-year-old, white-haired Volney Davis was flown to St. Paul, Minnesota, to receive his hearing in the same federal courthouse where he had pleaded guilty and been sentenced back in 1935. The hearing lasted six days, from July 7 to July 12, 1954. Witnesses included the original judge at his 1935 trial, G-man Melvin Purvis and his old flame, Edna Murray.

Volney's lawyers argued three points: that he did not know about his constitutional right to counsel, that he did not waive his right and that he was led to believe he would be given a short sentence if he entered a plea of guilty. Davis not only contended that his rights hadn't been explained clearly but also that he wasn't coherent enough at the time to understand them even if they had been. He claimed that when arrested in 1935, he was hit on the head by something (he had no idea what), that a gun was fired frighteningly near to him and that he was questioned relentlessly for long periods while constantly being guarded closely. And to top it off, the plane flying him from Chicago to Minneapolis had had some scary difficulties at Madison, Wisconsin. All these traumas caused him to be unable to make any intelligent or competent decisions by the time he was delivered to authorities in St. Paul.

The judge bought none of it, ruling that the original 1935 life sentence was upheld. He cited that there was ample evidence Davis had known exactly what he was doing when he pleaded guilty without a lawyer. Several FBI agents testified that while being questioned in 1935, Davis had admitted that he knew the FBI "had the goods" on him. The 1935 letter he had sent to his family from the Ramsey County jail was also quoted. In it he had told his loved ones, "I am here in jail and have entered a plea of guilty to conspiring in this case....I will be sentenced on Friday this week, I don't know what I will get but I expect it will be a life sentence. I guess I will be sent to the Government prison out in California, but before I go there I will be held for thirty days in some prison here."

Once again, Volney Davis left St. Paul sentenced to spend the rest of his life locked up. He would have gone back to prison even if had won his appeal, as there was still the matter of his conviction for the murder of Sheriff Sherrill during that 1923 holdup in Oklahoma. In 1957, three years after his appeal, he finally caught a break when the governor of Oklahoma granted him a parole from his murder conviction. He was then transferred to Leavenworth to finish out his life sentence for the Bremer kidnapping. Davis was relieved to finally be away from Alcatraz and Alvin Karpis. Then, on August 4, 1959, after serving twenty-four years in prison, he was given a parole due to his good behavior. Upon release, he went to work at a print shop in California, keeping his nose clean, just as he had promised his family he would in that 1935 letter he had written to them from the St. Paul jail. He even found love again, marrying Daisy Irene Graham on May 21, 1960. He finally attained complete freedom on June 9, 1966, when President Lyndon Johnson granted him a pardon.

AFTER A HARD LIFE of smoking and drinking, followed by twenty-four years in the country's harshest prisons, Volney Davis was in pretty poor health, suffering from hardening of the arteries. He died at age seventy-seven on July 20, 1979, in Sonoma County, California, after a brief bout of pneumonia. He is buried in Sebastopol, California, just sixty-five miles north of where his old flame and partner in crime Edna "the Kissing Bandit" Murray is buried in San Francisco.

When running with the Karpis-Barker Gang, Volney Davis appeared to have had no second thoughts about robbing, beating up people and kidnapping. In the documentary *Gangsterland*, Pam Paden Tippet offered her opinion on what made Davis and her grandmother Edna behave this way: "To treat people that way, you'd have to be a little weird. And they all drank a lot. I think they were drunk most of the time." But unlike his sweetheart, Edna Murray, Volney Davis did not look back fondly on the choices he'd made. In the end, unlike Alvin Karpis, he came to regret his life of crime.

OTHER GANG MEMBERS

The founders and core of the gang were always Alvin Karpis and Freddie Barker. Even Doc was not as important as the two desperados from whom the gang took its name. Volney Davis, Larry DeVol and Edna Murray were important members of the gang throughout their careers. But over the years, many other people came and went. Of those, there were three who played major roles.

Fred "Shotgun George Ziegler" Goetz

Ziegler's story is a sad one of potential wasted. His real name was Fred Goetz. He was born in Chicago on February 14, 1897, and showed great promise as a young man. Handsome and athletic, he graduated from the University of Illinois with a degree in engineering in 1918. He enlisted in the army and became a pilot in the army's Aviation Branch, rising to become a second lieutenant.

It was after World War I ended that things began to go wrong for Fred. While working as a lifeguard, he was charged with the attempted rape of a seven-year-old girl. The charge does seem out of character, as there was no indication over the rest of his life that he was either a pedophile or a sexual predator. However, he must have felt that he would be found guilty, because he left town, forfeiting the $5,000 in bail money.

Adopting the name of "Shotgun George Ziegler," he embarked on a career of bootlegging and robbery, culminating with his participation in Al Capone's plan to rub out the Bugs Moran Gang in what would become known as the St. Valentine's Day Massacre. It happened on February 14, 1929, which was Ziegler's thirty-second birthday. He took credit for engineering several of the details of the massacre, such as arriving in a vehicle dressed up to look like a patrol car and putting a few of the killers in police uniforms. He worked for Al Capone frequently, but he moved between gangs with ease.

He joined the Karpis-Barker Gang in time to be part of the Hamm kidnapping. He participated in the Swift Payroll robbery and reluctantly agreed to be part of the Bremer kidnapping. He created quite a stir when the gang was living on Bald Eagle Lake in White Bear Township, Minnesota, when the neighbors noticed that he had an unfortunate habit of sunbathing out on the lawn totally naked.

His personality was an enigma. Melvin Purvis described him as "well mannered, always polite, he was capable of generous kindness and conscienceless cruelty." He was a good friend to Byron Bolton and a good husband to his wife, Irene.

He died from shotgun wounds to the face on March 20, 1934, coming out of The Minerva, a restaurant in Chicago. The murder was never solved, but there are several possibilities. One theory is that he was shot by the Karpis-Barker Gang because he was talking too freely. It could also have been a member of Bugs Moran's gang taking revenge, or a member of Al Capone's gang because they feared he would reveal other participants in the St. Valentine's Day Massacre. The murder remains unsolved to this day.

Irene was so unhinged by his death that she was committed to a sanitarium in Chicago. While there, she became an FBI informant, even though the gang gave her part of proceeds from the Bremer kidnapping because she was Ziegler's widow.

Byron Bolton

Bolton's story is inextricably tied with Ziegler's, and it is also a sad one. If he hadn't met Ziegler, Bolton might have lived an honest, uneventful life. He was born on March 3, 1898, in Franklin, Illinois, and started his adult life as a farmer and then a businessman who was a partner in one of the very first car rental agencies. He also served in the U.S. Navy. But he was struggling to make a living when he met Ziegler in Chicago, where they often golfed together.

Between the two, Ziegler was the one with the brains. Bolton was described by the FBI as Ziegler's stooge. He certainly looked the part with his stocky build, heavy dark eyebrows and morose face. Ziegler recruited him to be a lookout for the St. Valentine's Day Massacre. Bolton was to give the signal when Bugs Moran showed up at the North Clark Street garage. Unfortunately, Bolton gave the signal too soon, as Moran was still a block away and escaped. Capone blamed Bolton for not getting Moran and wanted Bolton killed. Ziegler felt responsible for Bolton's predicament and sent him up north to stay out of Capone's way. Bolton lost his navy pension while in hiding, but Ziegler sent him money on a regular basis.

Bolton joined the Karpis-Barker Gang at the same time as Ziegler. Shortly after the Hamm kidnapping, Byron Bolton decided to fly to St. Paul from Chicago to pass off some hot bonds. He got the shock of his life when one of his fellow passengers on the plane turned out to be William Hamm Jr. Although they had been careful to keep Hamm's eyes covered during the entire kidnapping, Bolton was terrified that Hamm would recognize him, so much so that Bolton bolted from the plane when it made a quick stop in Madison, Wisconsin. The kidnapper found an alternate way to get to St. Paul from there.

He was captured by the FBI in the raid that killed Russell "Slim Gray" Gibson. It was the same day that Doc Barker was apprehended just a few blocks away, January 8, 1935. Brought back to St. Paul to stand trial for the Bremer kidnapping, he decided to plead guilty and become a cooperating witness. Perhaps Bolton agreed to be a witness because his connection to the Karpis-Barker Gang was Ziegler, and now that Ziegler was gone, Bolton felt no loyalty. He was also in ill health, suffering from tuberculosis. He ended up becoming the best witness the FBI had in the Bremer kidnapping trial.

Bolton claimed that he had not participated in the Bremer kidnapping, but he admitted that he knew about it, and even visited the house where Bremer was held. He was such a good witness that he received a very light sentence of only three to five years. After serving only three years, he and his wife, Vera, moved to California. He lived quietly, working as a salesman at a furniture store, under his real first name of William (Byron was his middle name). He died in March 1977 of natural causes, one of the few gang members to have that distinction. Perhaps his story is not all that sad in the end after all.

Charlie "Big Fitz" Fitzgerald

Charles Fitzgerald was an older member of the gang, born on March 16, 1877. He was only in his fifties, but so many gangsters died young or went to prison that he was not typical. He was noted as a dapper dresser and looked more like a banker or a businessman than a thug. The gang took advantage of that by using him to lure William Hamm to their car during the kidnapping in 1933. Karpis would later say that Charles handled his role perfectly, calling the performance a "masterpiece."

Charles was wounded in the hip during the robbery of the Swift Packing Company payroll in South St. Paul in August 1933.

According to the *New York Daily News*, Alvin Karpis specifically attempted to clear Peifer's name when he stated at his own sentencing that Peifer had nothing to do with the kidnapping of William Hamm. Charles Fitzgerald, sentenced at the same time as Karpis, also testified that Jack had nothing to do with the kidnapping and that the testimony of Byron Bolton was fabricated to get a better deal for himself. Karpis would later verify that Peifer not only *was* part of the plot, but that he indeed had initiated the idea. "How would you boys like to work on a kidnapping?" was what Peifer asked them. Further, Karpis noted that Peifer suggested the victim and helped plan the whole affair in exchange for a 10 percent cut of the expected $100,000 ransom.

The *New York Daily News* described Charles as one of Karpis's lieutenants in the gang, with a forty-year record in crime. Sentenced to life at the same time as Alvin, he was sent to Levenworth Prison. But he was only there a short time, as he was transferred to Alcatraz on August 6, 1936. He died on January 9, 1945. According to several newspaper articles, he died at Leavenworth, so he must have been transferred back there at some time. The official cause of death was a heart attack.

PART IV

THE END OF AN ERA

DEATH IN FLORIDA

The house on Lake Weir was perfect for Ma and Freddie. It wasn't huge, but it was certainly big enough. Two stories tall with four bedrooms on the second floor, it had a screened porch extending across the entire front of the house and overlooking the lake. Most important, it was extremely private, located in the small town of Ocklawaha, in the wilds of central Florida, not far from Ocala. The town itself was a wide spot in the road, barely even a village—just a few vacation homes, a post office and a gas station. The house was barely visible from the road, surrounded by huge live oaks covered with Spanish moss.

The cottage belonged to Carson Bradford, who had built it as a vacation home in 1930. He even gave it a name, Belle Air. In November 1934, through a friend, Joe Adams, he agreed to rent it to a Mrs. Blackburn, whom he had never met. He was reluctant to rent it out at first because his family enjoyed going there themselves, but the amount of money offered was just too good to pass up. Of course, his new renter was Ma Barker, and she was willing to pay $75 per month. Furthermore, she would pay the first and last month's rent in advance and in cash. She paid the $150 to Adams with three $50 bills that came from the ransom money for the Bremer kidnapping.

They moved into the cottage on November 7, 1934. It was a nice little family. Mrs. Blackburn had two "sons" with her. One of them was her actual son Freddie, while the other was gang member Harry Campbell.

The Barker house on Lake Weir. *Photo by Deborah Frethem.*

In his book *G-Men, Gangsters and Gators,* Brian Hunt described the reaction of the neighbors to the arrival of this unusual trio. Frank Barber, who kept an eye on the house when it was vacant, said he didn't find them suspicious at all. He tried to get to know them a little, thinking they were just business associates of Bradford's. Mrs. Westberry, who lived just to the east, thought the group acted "rather queerly." She did not like Wynona Burdette, Campbell's girlfriend, when she arrived later.

Before Burdette's arrival, Campbell had been busy flirting with Mrs. Sexton, a married woman who lived in the small cottage on the same property. He would often visit when Mr. Sexton was at work. He took Mrs. Sexton out to dinner, tried to get her to drink with him and pressured her to have sex with him. When she refused, the Blackburns complained to their landlord that the occupants of the cottage were "annoying" them. Bradford told the Sextons they had to leave. He wasn't going to risk the seventy-five dollars per month he was getting for the main house to preserve the mere eight dollars he was getting from the Sextons. Willie Woodbury, the caretaker and gardener Ma had hired, moved into the cottage with his wife.

In December, Freddie got word that Alvin Karpis was in Miami. He drove down to meet with him, and then later he and Ma drove down together.

During this second meeting, they planned the robbery of an armored car in Cleveland. Karpis, Freddie and Harry drove up to Cleveland but decided that the town was too hot for them to successfully pull off the heist. Karpis visited the cottage upon their return to Florida. He was impressed by the setup and described the scene in his autobiography: "It was a gorgeous layout. The cottage sat fifty yards from the lake, and it came with a boathouse and a launch....It was a small paradise, and Ma had the luxury of a maid and a gardener." Karpis stayed with Ma and Freddie for a few days and did some fishing. He said that Ma was a changed woman in Florida, that she had mellowed and seemed relaxed and happy. When Karpis left, Ma gave him a Christmas present for the baby that he and Delores Delaney were expecting.

On New Year's Day, Doc visited the cottage. He was still interested in pulling off the job in Cleveland, despite the assessment of Karpis and Freddie that the town was too hot. Doc and Freddie drove to Miami to visit Karpis again, and he now was satisfied that the heist could be carried off successfully. Doc agreed to go up north to get everything set up. He was uncertain if he would be able to find the lake house again once he left. He got a Florida road map and circled the town so he could be sure to remember the name. He said he would send a letter when everything was set.

Ma was not the only one happy in Florida. Freddie was enjoying the fishing and boating, often going out on the lake with some of their friendly neighbors. On one of these trips, his new friends told him about a legendary alligator who was called "Big Joe," "Gator Joe" or sometimes "Old Joe." According to W.D. Smith in *An American Crime Family*, Freddie became obsessed with the creature, which was supposed to be not only huge but also the oldest alligator in the area. Freddie killed a hog that he had purchased from a local farmer and began to take long boat rides on Lake Weir, towing the carcass of the hog behind as bait, hoping to lure the creature near enough that he could shoot him with his Tommy gun.

This little piece of tranquility was not to last. In the very early morning of January 16, 1935, fourteen FBI agents arrived in three cars, led by Special Agent E.L. Connelly. They surrounded the house and ordered Freddie Barker to surrender.

The FBI had found out where Ma and Freddie were hiding through a combination of luck and good police work. Doc Barker and Byron Bolton had been captured in Chicago on January 8, 1935. They were held in the Cook County jail and interrogated for more than twenty-four hours without a break. They were given no food and kept in the clothes they were wearing

The boathouse on Lake Weir. *Photo by Deborah Frethem.*

at the time of capture. These tactics were commonplace in that era, although they certainly would not be allowed today.

What the FBI most wanted to know was the whereabouts of the other members of the gang. Arthur wasn't talking, but eventually Bolton broke under the pressure. He told the FBI that he wasn't exactly sure where Freddie Barker was, but he knew, from conversations that he had overheard, that he was staying in a house on a lake in the middle of Florida. He wasn't sure of either the name of the lake or the name of the town, but he remembered that Freddie was doing a lot of hunting and fishing and was amusing himself by hunting a legendary alligator named "Old Joe." He described Freddie dragging the pig carcass behind his boat to try and catch the gator.

Connelly wasn't sure whether to believe Bolton. It sounded like a pretty fantastic story, and Bolton was certainly fuzzy on the details. But a few days later, he looked at the maps that had been found in Doc's apartment. One had the town of Ocala circled; another had circled a chain of lakes. It looked very much like Bolton had been telling the truth, so Connelley and other special agents headed down to Florida.

They began serious investigative work by asking questions and scouting the area. Of the lakes in the chain, Lake Weir seemed the most likely, as it was the largest. They drove the roads around the lake, and trawled along the shoreline in a rented fishing boat. They got a big break when Connelley went to talk to the postmaster of Ocklawaha, J.T. Greenlee. Although he did not recognize the photos of Alvin Karpis or Freddie Barker, Greenlee did mention that there was only one place being rented out at that time. He said the people living there were the Blackburns. Connelley knew that this was an alias used by Freddie Barker. On the morning of January 14, 1935, a special agent strolled out on a public dock on Lake Weir. He started fishing in the lake and waited. A barefoot man came out of the two-story house a few feet away. He walked out and started a conversation with the agent. This was Freddie Barker, and the agent knew it. They had found their man.

The raid was meticulously planned. Connelley wanted no mistakes. He began by making a drawing of the property and the layout of all the buildings, the dock and the lakeshore. He added circles to indicate the trees on the property. He intended to capture them alive, just as he had done with Byron Bolton and Doc Barker in Chicago a week before, but he was prepared to use deadly force if necessary.

Earl Connelley, like many of Hoover's new men, did not have a law enforcement background. He had studied law and accounting and joined the FBI in 1920, working his way up through the ranks. Hoover sent him to Chicago in December 1934 and placed him in charge of the investigation of the activities of the Karpis-Barker Gang.

Harry Campbell and Wynona Burdette were not at the house. They were in Miami visiting with Alvin Karpis and had planned to drive back to the lake house on the night of January 15. At the last moment, Harry decided that he wanted one more day of fishing, so they delayed their trip to Ocklawaha. That most likely saved their lives.

Just before dawn on the sixteenth, the agents surrounded the house. Accounts of the following events vary in some details. Some accounts say that Connelley knocked on the door. Other records indicate that he merely shouted, "We are Federal agents of the Division of Investigation, United States Department of Justice! Come out with your hands up and you will not be harmed, provided you do as instructed. Otherwise, we will use tear gas and drive you out!" One of the other agents present remembered it rather differently. Instead of this very formal declaration, Connelley simply said, "Come on out, Freddie, we are Department of Justice agents and have the house surrounded."

Freddie Barker did not respond to the demand to surrender, and a gun battle ensued. Witnesses said that the FBI agents just kept firing until all their ammunition had been exhausted, not even paying attention as to whether return fire was still coming from inside the house. Between two thousand and three thousand rounds were pumped into the house. The air was full of tear gas, as some of the canisters the FBI threw at the house did not go in the windows and instead bounced out on the grass, blinding the agents themselves.

According to official records, shots came from inside the house, and no agents fired their guns until after they were fired upon. Further, these records report that shots were coming from two different locations within the house at the same time, which would indicate that both people inside must have been firing weapons. There is no way of knowing for certain if this is what transpired or if these records were deliberately written that way to justify the killing of an "elderly" woman in her own home.

There was a witness to the entire event who was not a member of the FBI team. The caretaker, Willie Woodberry, who had moved into the cottage on the property, and his wife were present during the whole event. He was interviewed by the *Tampa Tribune* in 1963, and although many years had passed, his memories seemed to be very vivid.

Willie was twenty-six years old in 1936. He and his wife were awakened by the demand from the FBI to come out with hands in the air. Willie believed that his employers were "rich tourists" and had no idea that they were criminals. Therefore, he assumed that the shouted threat came from robbers intent on stealing money from the Blackburns.

"Then the bullets came a-whizzin' past my head," he said in the *Tampa Tribune* interview, "and I was so scared that my knees were knocking." He and his wife dove underneath their bed for cover. Neither one was hit by flying bullets.

When everything was finally quiet at around 11:30 a.m., the agents asked Willie Woodberry to go inside and check out the house. He was understandably reluctant at first, but the agents gave him twenty dollars and the Barkers did know him and would probably not have harmed him. In fact, they were beyond the ability to harm anyone. Willie found their bodies.

Official records indicate that both bodies were in the southwest bedroom. Ma had been killed by three shots to the chest, one of which went through her heart. She was barefoot and wearing a house dress, and she had a Thompson submachine in her hand. Freddie was face-down in the middle of the room. A Thompson submachine gun lay near his right hand, where he had dropped it as he fell. He was so riddled with bullets that his shirt had been torn to pieces.

Woodberry remembered it somewhat differently. He said that Ma had been shot through the head and that he found Fred's body in her lap, that she had been trying to staunch his wounds when she was killed. He also reported that there was blood everywhere. He did not say anything about any weapon being found either in Ma's hand or near her body.

One of the agents was interviewed years later. He admitted that they were only after Freddie Barker that day. They did not consider his mother a criminal at that time.

Of course, agents searched the house. They found a large cache of weapons and just over $14,000 in cash. Doc Barker's letter to his brother was found under a cloth on a living room table. The room in which the bodies were found had 147 bullet holes, and much damage had been done to the house itself. The agents estimated that walls, ceiling and several windows would have to be replaced. The Bradfords did receive some compensation for the damage done to their cottage. In February, they opened the house to the crowds of people who "continued to come and beg to be admitted." They charged fifty cents per person and put out a sign in front of the house that said, "Crime Doesn't Pay."

The day following the shootout, a coroner's jury in Ocala ruled officially that Arizona and Freddie Barker had been shot to death while "resisting arrest" and that the FBI agents were acting in self-defense and the interest of preserving their own lives. Ironically, one year to the day after the Bremer kidnapping, the FBI was officially exonerated for the deaths in Ocklawaha.

The bodies were taken to Pyles' mortuary in nearby Ocala. They remained there for several months, due to a dispute over what to do with them. Initially, the FBI put the embalmed bodies on display, hoping that the other gang members would appear to verify the death of their friends. They were particularly hoping to capture Alvin Karpis in this manner, but he did not appear. The public came, however. Ten to fifteen thousand people viewed the bodies.

However, there is an interesting postscript to the incident. The very next day, George Barker, Ma's husband and father of the four boys, reentered the picture. He asked for the bodies and personal effects of his wife and son. He got no response. In late January, he filed suit against the federal government for the money that had been found in the house on Lake Weir after the gun battle, which amounted to almost $15,000. He claimed that there was no proof that the money was from criminal activity and therefore it should not have been confiscated. Surprisingly, he won the case, and after expenses and lawyer's fees, he received $1,200 and the right to claim the bodies of his wife and son. Ma and Freddie were laid to rest on September 25, 1935, more than eight months after their death. They are buried at Williams Timberhill Cemetery in Oklahoma. Neither of them has a tombstone, just small markers. Freddie's says, "Let us not forget He who gave us life understands all of the reasons." Ma's inscription reads, "The darkest night shall end in a bright day." George openly wept during the graveside service.

George Barker died on April 30, 1941. Of his four sons, only Lloyd, who was living in Denver, Colorado, survived him.

In 2016, the cottage was ferried to the Canary Island Recreation and Conservation Area. It is to be turned into a museum. As for the alligator that helped the FBI track down the Barkers, he was killed in 1956.

At the time of the shootout in Ocklawaha, Alvin Karpis was still a free man but on the run. There would be more arrests, more trials and more deaths, but effectively, the career of the gang ended there on the shores of Lake Weir. Former Orlando police chief and Barker historian Lee McGehee noted, "1933 was the year of the gangster in the United States, 1934 was the year of the death of the gangster in the United States."

THE END OF THE SYSTEM

By 1934, efforts to clean up the corruption in St. Paul were underway, led by crusading *St. Paul Daily News* editor Howard Kahn, Public Safety Commissioner Gus Barfuss and reform police chief Thomas Dahill, an honest, dedicated public servant. Upon succeeding Tom Brown in 1932, Dahill declared, "Gangsters and would be gangsters are not wanted here, and we intend to do everything in our power to drive them out." To that end, he began making arrests of the formerly protected criminals. But once again, good ideas can have unintended consequences. Harry Sawyer had kept the bad guys in line within St. Paul. But if the police weren't holding up their end of the bargain, why should Harry and his friends honor theirs?

That seemed to give the green light to the Karpis-Barker Gang to carry out the two most profitable crimes of their careers, the William Hamm and Edward Bremer kidnappings, which ultimately brought about their undoing. With these two direct assaults carried out on important citizens

A vintage 1932 Ford travels down a gravel road in rural Hampton. Minnesota. Taken during the filming of the documentary movie *Gangsterland*, co-produced by Cynthia Schreiner Smith and Bick Smith. *Photo by Sharon Johnson.*

within St. Paul, the tide of public opinion turned against the O'Connor System. The city began electing public officials who were determined to clean up corruption.

Editor Kahn and several prominent businessmen raised money to fund a plan to clean up their city. To execute it, they hired agent Wallace Ness Jamie, a university-trained criminologist and nephew of Eliot Ness. Ness and his group of "Untouchables" had brought down Al Capone by tapping his phones and sending him off to Alcatraz for tax evasion. Apparently, wiretapping skills ran in the Ness family. Starting in the spring of 1934, Jamie secretly set up wiretaps in the Public Safety Building. He found a closet in the police headquarters where all the phone lines came together, sneaking into it almost daily for a month to listen in on phone calls, recording them on an early form of wiretapping machine called a pamograph. He recorded more than 2,500 hours of conversations. After a yearlong investigation, the *St. Paul Daily News* published an exposé on the corruption within the department on July 24, 1935, resulting in the dismissal and indictment of twenty-one police officials. Big Tom Brown was not one of them. He had cleverly made all of his covert calls from his office at the St. Paul Hotel.

While the recordings did not hold enough evidence to arrest Brown, another conversation at the city's Federal Courts Building did finally lead to his suspension. Several Karpis-Barker Gang members were on trial in 1935 for the Bremer kidnapping. Byron Bolton testified that Brown had allegedly received a large portion of Hamm's ransom. The FBI came calling for Brown to appear in court, but he was conveniently working "out of town" and could not be reached.

In the midst of the investigations in 1934, Thomas Dahill became assistant inspector of detectives when he was replaced as chief by St. Paul's newly elected mayor. Dahill continued to arrest gangsters, but unfortunately, in June 1936, he was caught up in the confusion of the corruption scandal and was suspended. Although Dahill was eventually cleared of wrongdoing, he resigned from the department on July 7, 1936.

Despite Tom Brown's refusal to testify, there was plenty of circumstantial evidence that he was in cahoots with gangsters. Much of it was provided by Tom Dahill, who supplied plausible links between the Karpis-Barker Gang and his predecessor when he testified during the Bremer kidnapping trials. Brown was suspended from the police department on July 17, 1936. His appeal of the dismissal fell flat with the review board, again thanks to testimony from Dahill. Brown was officially fired from the St. Paul police force on October 9, 1936. However, he never faced any charges for his part in Hamm's kidnapping because the three-year statute of limitations had expired. He also never faced consequences for any of his other misdeeds. Apparently, he still had enough influential friends that enabled him to freely skate away. But with the dismissal of Tom Brown, the era of the O'Connor system came to an end. No longer protected, the criminals scattered, leaving their once "safe haven" behind.

Tom Dahill subsequently ran a restaurant for ten years on Jackson Street in downtown St. Paul, later opening a lunch counter in the Lowry Medical Arts Building. He died at age sixty-nine in 1960 and is buried at Calvary Cemetery.

Tom Brown left St. Paul for a life of obscurity in Morris, a small city in west-central Minnesota. Although he left in disgrace, he did not leave penniless. His partnerships with gangsters had netted him a tidy sum. Karpis-Barker Gang member Larry DeVol claimed that he personally gave Harry Sawyer $100 per week, which was then passed on to Tom Brown for protection. In addition, DeVol reported that 10 percent of all Karpis-Barker robbery money went to Brown. Ironically, Tom Brown took the money he earned during Prohibition and opened a liquor store in Morris. But it seems he didn't completely give up his unethical ways. Evidently, he had not reported all the sales at his store and had paid no taxes. He disappeared after being forewarned that he was to be charged with violating federal liquor laws. Brown eventually turned himself in, working out a deal that cost him a year in prison and a $3,500 fine. After his release, Brown settled in the small town of Ely, Minnesota, near the Canadian border and opened up another liquor store, Brown's Bottle Shop.

Tom Brown continued to deny that he had been a corrupt cop until the day he died of a heart attack while on a walk in January 1959. He was sixty-nine years old. He is buried next to his wife, Mary, at the Ely Cemetery.

AFTER THE BREMER KIDNAPPING, Harry Sawyer was held briefly by the St. Paul police, but he was released on February 7, 1934, as authorities were satisfied that he was not involved. In November 1934, possibly sensing that there was trouble ahead, Harry and Gladys headed down to Long Beach, Mississippi. There he operated a gambling house, but the couple attracted attention with their lavish spending.

He was indicted in absentia for conspiring in the kidnapping of Edward Bremer after Wynona Burdette, the girlfriend of gang member Harry Campbell, testified against him. She stated at the 1935 trial of Doc Barker that Harry had been part of the plot. She said that planning meetings, which she had personally witnessed, had taken place at his home. A former maid at the Sawyer home identified the members of the Karpis-Barker Gang, including Karpis himself, as frequent visitors.

Harry was taken by federal agents on the coast of Mississippi on Friday, May 3, 1935. He was sitting in his parked car in front of his business when he was apprehended, and he did not resist arrest. He was taken to New Orleans to await transfer back to Minnesota for trial. He did not fight extradition. Gladys was also taken into custody; however, no charges were made against her, so she was released. His bond was set at $100,000, which was a huge amount of money, roughly equivalent to $1 million today.

When the trial began, Harry entered the courtroom, smiling and acknowledging his friends and the press corps. On the witness stand, he was the picture of confidence and bravado, claiming that he had nothing to do with the kidnapping, although he admitted to knowing the parties involved because they frequented the Green Lantern. He also said he had done business with Edward Bremer and his bank, and Edward and Adolph Bremer were both occasional customers as well. Bremer himself supported

Harry's claims, as he stated on the stand that he barely knew him, and he could not connect him to the kidnapping.

But the testimony of Edna Murray shook Harry, as she calmly testified about him attending meetings that took place in her apartment and a trip she took to his farm on the day of the kidnapping. Even more damning was the testimony of Byron Bolton, who told how the gang had only been considering robbing Bremer's bank and that it was Sawyer who had convinced them that the kidnapping was a better idea.

The jury found Sawyer guilty of "kidnapping and conspiring to transport" Edward Bremer on January 24, 1936. He spent most of his sentence in Alcatraz, where he worked in the prison kitchen.

Sawyer's wife, Gladys, was furious about her husband's conviction. After all, her lifestyle had changed drastically. She was no longer a queen in St. Paul, with wealth and status. She lived for a short time with Harry's parents in Nebraska but eventually found herself living in the back room of a grocery store in Omaha. She vowed that if Harry was going to prison, so was Tom Brown. She testified against Brown via deposition at his hearings, to no avail. Eventually, she went to California to be near her daughter. She

The large atrium of the Landmark Center, the original old federal courthouse. *Photo by Bick Smith.*

died in San Francisco from a heart attack following gall bladder surgery on November 15, 1969.

Sawyer had a tough time in Alcatraz. His prison doctors said he was overweight and had gonorrhea. He continued to claim that he was innocent and called Edna Murray and Byron Bolton liars. Despite interrogation by the FBI, he never gave information on his friends in St. Paul. Released from prison in 1955, he was desperately ill. He died on June 23, 1955, from cancer in a Chicago Hospital. He is buried at Westlawn Cemetery in Cook County, Illinois. His tombstone reads "Beloved Brother." Even bad guys have people who love them.

AS TIMES BEGAN TO change in St. Paul and things got too hot for Jack Peifer, he closed the club. On May 13, 1935, he married Violet Elizabeth Nordquist, his fashion model girlfriend, in South Dakota. It is probably not a coincidence that they decided to legalize their relationship at the same time he came under suspicion for the Hamm kidnapping. Now they could not testify against each other.

Several witnesses testified against him during his trial in 1936, including Frances Nash (widow of the gangster Frank Nash, who was killed in the Kansas City Massacre), former police chief Thomas Dahill, gang member Byron Bolton and Edward C. Bartholmey, the postmaster in Bensenville, Illinois, in whose home Hamm was held for the three days of his captivity. The prosecution alleged that Peifer received $10,000 from the ransom proceeds as a reward for his suggestion of the victim.

He was found guilty and sentenced to thirty years in prison on July 31, 1936. Witnesses said that he appeared distraught at the verdict. He was returned to his jail cell, and at 1:20 p.m. that day he was found dead, an apparent victim of poisoning. The immediate conclusion was that Jack had committed suicide. Eyewitnesses at the trial said that they had seen Jack pass a white handkerchief in front of his face and that he had a small white capsule in his hand.

The following day, the *Minneapolis Star* described the reaction of Violet, his "young and pretty wife." She asked to see his body and then stroked his hair. "Jack, dear," she said, "This is what you get for being so good to people."

An autopsy revealed the cause of death was potassium cyanide poisoning, and the official ruling was suicide. Violet later claimed that Jack would never have killed himself. He felt he was wrongly convicted and was sure he could win acquittal upon appeal. She always felt that he had been murdered, either by gangsters who were afraid of what he might say or by corrupt police officers who didn't want an appeal of his case.

Peifer is buried at Sunset Memorial Park Cemetery in Minneapolis. His daughter, Amy, left a touching message for him in 2009: "To a wonderful, strong, kind and dapper gentleman. May you be the bright light of heaven. I can't wait until the day I can see you smile again."

IN 1932, THE FEDERAL government began to investigate St. Paul's bootleg king, Leon Gleckman, for tax evasion. He was indicted and tried, but the result was a hung jury and a mistrial. It was discovered that one of the jurors in the trial, Bernard Fuchs, had been bribed by Leon's brother, Alexander, to find Leon not guilty. Leon was tried again in 1934. The government contended that he spent $115,082 during the years of 1929, 1930 and 1931 but had only declared income of $40,000 for that entire three years. He was found guilty and sentenced to eighteen months in prison and fined $10,000.

He arrived at Leavenworth Prison on March 28, 1936, as inmate no. 48710. Then he served another six-month sentence in the Minneapolis Workhouse for his complicity in the jury tampering.

After his release, he had very little time to enjoy his freedom, as he died in St. Paul on July 14, 1941, in a one-car accident. According to the *Minneapolis Star*, he was nearly decapitated when he crashed his car into a viaduct on Kellogg Boulevard near the Union Depot, after having "played golf with friends until dusk and spent the evening with friends." His blood alcohol content at the time was 0.23. How ironic that the "Bootleg King" died with that high a level of intoxication. Although the cause of death is officially an accident, there is speculation that it was not an accident at all but rather suicide, as he was facing another possible prison sentence for tax evasion. Is a day spent enjoying the company of friends consistent with suicide? It is impossible to know exactly what was going on in Gleckman's mind that day.

IN THE WAKE OF the O'Connor System, the St. Paul Police Department wanted to ensure that it would never have another chief like Big Tom Brown. Sweeping changes were made to overhaul the process of choosing a new police chief. Strict rules of conduct for all officers were also put in place to hopefully prevent such corruption from happening again. Those reforms are still in place today.

BIBLIOGRAPHY

Official Documents

Marriage Licenses of County of Joplin, Missouri, Joplin Missouri County Courthouse.

San Francisco, California Area Funeral Home Records 1895–1985. Ancestry.com.

Steenberg, Edward J. "Ed." John Joseph O'Connor and the "Layover Agreement." Information available at the St. Paul Police Historical Society.

United States Census 1850, 1860, 1870, 1910, 1920, 1930 and 1940. United Stated Federal Census Office.

U.S. Penitentiary, Alcatraz, California, Prison Index, 1934–63.

Volney Davis, Appellant, v. United Staes of America, Appellee. 226 F.2d 834 (8th Cir. 1955). Justice U.S. Law.

World War I Draft Registration Cards. Military Records, United States National Archives.

World War II Draft Registration Cards. Military Records, United States National Archives.

Websites

findagrave.com.

sangamonlink.com.

Documentary Videos

Alcatraz, Island of Hate. Asteron Productions, 1980.
Gangsterland. CyBick Productions, 2011.
Public Enemy #1: An Interview with the Notorious 1930s Crime Legend Alvin "Creepy" Karpis. Canadian Broadcasting Corporation, 1976.

Interviews by Authors

Kaphingst, Fred, Ed Steenberg and Jeff Neuberger. St. Paul Police Historians.
Livesey, Robert, coauthor of *On the Rock* by Alvin Karpis.
Tippet, Pam Paden, granddaughter of Edna Murray.

Books

Hunt, Brian. *G-Men, Gangsters and Gators: The FBI Flying Squad and the Deaths of Ma and Freddie Barker in Florida.* N.p.: self-published, Brian D. Hunt, 2012.
Karpis, Alvin, with Bill Trent. *Public Enemy Number One: The Alvin Karpis Story.* New York: Coward, McCann & Geoghegan Inc., 1971.
Karpis, Alvin, with Robert Livesey. *On the Rock.* Toronto, CAN: Musson Book Company, 1980.
Kazanjian, Howard, and Chris Enss. *Ma Barker, America's Most Wanted Mother.* Guilford, CT: TWODOT Publishing, 2017.
Maccabee, Paul. *John Dillinger Slept Here: A Crooks' Tour of Crime and Corruption in St. Paul, 1920–1936.* St. Paul: Minnesota Historical Society Press, 1995.
Mahoney, Tim. *Secret Partners: Big Tom Brown and the Barker Gang.* St. Paul: Minnesota Historical Society Press, 2013.
Paden Tippet, Pam. *Run Rabbit Run: The Edna Murray Story.* N.p.: CreateSpace Independent Publishing Platform, 2013.
Smith, W.D. *The Barker-Karpis Gang: An American Crime Family.* N.p.: self-published, 2016.
Thompson, Julie A. *The Hunt for the Last Public Enemy in Northeastern Ohio: Alvin "Creepy" Karpis and His Road to Alcatraz.* Charleston, SC: The History Press, 2019.
Whitehead, Don. *The FBI Story: A Report to the People.* New York: Random House, 1956.
Wingerd, Mary Lethert. *Claiming the City: Politics, Faith, and the Power of Place in Saint Paul.* Ithaca, NY: Cornell University Press, 2001.

Newspapers

Brainerd (MN) Daily Dispatch. "Dapper Danny Hogan Given Fine Funeral." December 7, 1928.

Chicago Tribune. "Gang Murder Bares Strange Tale of Crime." March 22, 1934.

Fort Scott (KS) Daily Tribune. "Fear a Jail Break." July 22, 1921.

Hammond Times (Munster IN). "Wife Slays Last of Ma Barker's Sons." March 22, 1949.

Joplin (MO) Globe. "Bandit Believed Barker Ends His Life at Wichita." August 30, 1927.

LaCrosse (WI) Tribune. "Danny Hogan Held Here in Staats Death." December 6, 1928.

Lincoln (NE) Star. "Hold Former Lincoln Man in Kidnapping." May 4, 1935.

Lincoln (NE) Star Journal. "Asked Death for Husband's Crime." September 27, 1927.

Miami (OK) Daily News-Record. "Bandit's Widow Gets Two to Four Years." September 27, 1927.

———. "Barker Slides to Liberty from Arkansas Jail." March 31, 1927.

———. "Kidnap Suspect Held in Jail." February 7, 1935.

Minneapolis Star Tribune. "Barker Gang Girl on Stand." May 2, 1935.

———. "Bremer Held Captive Three Weeks." February 8, 1934, 12.

———. "Bremer Kidnap Fugitive Found." February 8, 1935.

———. "Bremer Kidnaping Prisoner Escapes from Federal Man." February 7, 1935.

———. "Detective Tale Gives Clues to Gangster Plot." April 29, 1932.

———. "Doc Barker's Moll Says He Protected Her." April 26, 1935.

———. "Fuchs Admits Guilt in Gleckman Case." April 14, 1937.

———. "Gang Wanted in Bremer Case Escapes Raid." September 7, 1934.

———. "Gleckman Convicted: Gets 18 Months Term." November 29, 1934.

———. "G-Men Kill a Mother." August 14, 1936.

———. "Leon Gleckman Challenges US to Arrest Him." May 20, 1932.

———. "Prosecution in Gleckman Tax Case Rests." November 20, 1934.

———. "Sawyer, Barker, Karpis Put to Work at Alcatraz." September 5, 1936.

———. "Second Bandit Victim Dies." December 17, 1932.

———. "Suspended in Police Investigation." June 25, 1935.

———. "US May Enter Peifer Suicide Poison Inquiry." August 1, 1936.

Neosho (MO) Daily News. "Geo. Barker Dies." March 1, 1941.

New York Daily News. "A Haven for Criminals." April 8, 1934.

———. "Karpis Gets Life." July 28, 1936.

Saint Cloud (MN) Times. "Bolton Story to Be Placed Before Court." July 16, 1936.

———. "Four Persons Detained in Bank Robbery Probe." December 17, 1932.

Saint Paul (MN) Globe. "Next Chief of Police." June 3, 1900.

Salt Lake Telegram. "Murdered Man Listed as Ma Barker's Son." March 22, 1949.

Salt Lake Tribune. "Outlaw's Widow Asserts Husband Killed Sheriff." September 20, 1927.

San Francisco Examiner. Obituaries. November 16, 1969.

St. Louis Post-Dispatch. "St. Paul Gang Leader Slain by Bomb Car." December 5, 1928.

Tampa Bay Times. "Tiny Town Owes Status to Celebrated Gangster." January 15, 1992.

Tampa Tribune. "Ma Barkers Last Stand." July 28, 1963.

———. "More than $10,000 Found on Slain Pair." January 18, 1935.

ABOUT THE AUTHORS

CYNTHIA SCHREINER SMITH is an actor/writer/producer born and raised in St. Paul, Minnesota, where she still lives in a suburb outside the city. This is her first book, but she has published short pieces on St. Paul history in the *St. Paul Almanac* in 2012 and 2014. Since 1998, she has worked as a tour guide for Down in History Tours in St. Paul, researching and writing scripts for their historical tours. She is best known there for performing the St. Paul Gangster Tour as Karpis-Barker Gang member Edna Murray, the Kissing Bandit. Cynthia and her husband, Bick Smith, are co-owners of CyBick Productions, producing corporate videos and short films. In 2011, they produced *Gangsterland*, a documentary-style movie about 1930s gangsters in St. Paul.

DEBORAH FRETHEM previously published *Ghost Stories of St. Petersburg, Clearwater and Pinellas County* with The History Press in 2007; *Haunted Tampa: Spirits of the Bay* in 2013; and *Haunted Ybor City* in 2014. She has also written scripts for historical tours in Minnesota and Florida and conducted these tours for more than twenty years. She has a bachelor's degree in history from Olaf College and has served as tour manager for Down in History Tours in St. Paul. She is currently a writer and storyteller, living on a boat in the Mississippi River in downtown St. Paul.

Visit us at
www.historypress.com
·······································